*The Garden of Love and Loss*

# The Garden of Love and Loss

## A YEAR-LONG SPIRITUAL GUIDE
## THROUGH GRIEF

## Judith Sarah Schmidt, Ph.D.

*Full Court Press*
*Englewood Cliffs, New Jersey*

*First Edition*

Copyright © 2020 by Judith Sarah Schmidt

Published in the United States of America
by Full Court Press, 601 Palisade Avenue,
Englewood Cliffs, NJ 07632
*fullcourtpress.com*

ISBN 978-1-946989-79-6
Library of Congress Control Number: 2020918013

*Book design by Barry Sheinkopf*

*Cover art by Leigh Rosoff*

To my daughter Leslie
*Your spirit lights my way.*

*To my dear friends, family, patients, and students,*
*my gratitude to you each for the sacred honor*
*of sitting with you in your grief*
*and learning with you*
*how precious is the life of a single tear.*

"Where am I, I don't know, I'll never know, in the silence, in the silence you don't know, you must go on, I can't go on, I'll go on."

—Samuel Beckett, *The Unnamable*

# Table Of Contents

# Introduction

THERE IS A TALE. . .OF A MOTHER whose child lies ill and dying. She visits the wise elder of the village to ask him to save her child. He tells her, "Your child will be saved when you are given a tiny mustard seed by someone in this village who lives in a house in which no one has died."

The desperate mother travels from house to house, knocking at each door and begging,

"Please, if no one has died in this house, give me a mustard seed that my little one may be healed."

At each house, she hears again and again:

"Here a father has died,"

"Here our mother is dead,"

"Here our grandmother is dead,"

"Here we have lost our child."

She returns to the wise man and tells him someone has died in every house. The wise man tells the heartbroken mother: "That is all I can give you—the solace of knowing you are not alone."

Yes, each one of us, you and you and you, and I, each sit alone with our broken heart. And yet, because we can know and touch and be touched by our own brokenness, we grow able to turn to meet the broken heart of the other. We give and receive the comfort of solace, from one another and from the invisible mystery that creates all that is.

# Dear Reader

I T IS HARD TO IMAGINE. Once upon a time, we were children, who knew nothing about death and dying. We lived in a sort of Garden of Eden, where it seemed the Tree of Life would blossom forever.

And then arrives the loss of a loved one. We each come to know loss and grief in our own way: A loved one dies suddenly in an auto or plane crash, or from a heart attack, from cancer, or by suicide, or at war. You may live through the long, slow progression of losing a loved one to dementia, and grieve through the stations of loss: of memory, of no longer recognizing your face, of slowly disappearing—gone before dying.

Each of us will, in our own way, come to live in a garden in which we turn and turn the soil of our heartbreak and are turned by it. We are bent low in the darkness of our grief. Silence envelops our garden, mutes our senses, mutes our aliveness. Our heart falls into a shroud of silence. Sometimes we wonder: Will we ever be moved, ever be touched by life again?

The answer is a distant, yet-to-be-found *Yes.*

The question, "Will life ever touch me again?" will be lived by each of us along our journey through the Land of Grief. Some of us may find ourselves wandering in a desert of emptiness. Life waits beyond what we can imagine as we journey—exiled in the lifeless wilderness of our soul—without any map.

Somewhere, somehow, along our way, we begin to sense life coming to us again. Unexpectedly, we will hear, and we will cherish awakening to the song of a bird calling us to a new day. Over time, we begin to see with our heart how loss moves us through darkness toward a light more poignant than we have ever known.

Somehow, out of some mysterious process called life, and death, and loss, this dark time brings us some small dots of light, shows us a way to raise the shards of our grief upward toward sparks of life, toward the sounds and colors of life all around us. Somehow, along our way, we find the courage of spirit to plant flowers of living beside the ashes of our loss.

A deeper sense of wonder softly touches us and ever so delicately and slowly unwinds the shroud of silence. We sense something vast turning us and returning us slowly back toward life. We finally come to see our sojourn as one of both loss and life, not either-or, but both simultaneously.

Loss on one side of us, life on the other—companions gently guiding our broken heart onto a path of profound tenderness.

And so, no matter where we are, you in your loss, me in mine, we sit together in The Garden of Love and Loss, each of us initiated by our broken heart onto the sacred path of learning how to journey through grief toward living a true and tender life.

Little by little, we learn how to enter grief and how to live with it, never to get over it or move on without it. We learn one of the deepest lessons in life: how to accept and live with all that comes to us in this life—everything, the light and dark, the broken and whole, the love and the loss. On this journey, we learn we can and do live with everything. With hearts cracked wide open, we mutter our light and dark to one another, sing songs of grief for who and what we have lost, and offer praise for the force of life that pulses all around and within us.

Although your journey through the Land of Grief is one of broken heartedness, may you come to know your heart will also be touched and opened in unimaginable ways.  May you be visited not only by darkness but touched by a most poignant light.  May you know not only the deadness of stone but also a profound awakening to the sacredness of all life.

It is my deep hope that, through this book's journey, you take something with you to light your way, to help you see in the dark, something to carry and to pass on to others.

## *My Story*

I begin this book by sharing the story of my daughter Leslie's death, on Mother's Day, 1969, when she was four years old.

For weeks before Leslie became ill, she woke me every morning, put her head on my pillow, looked deep into my eyes, and sang me the same story:

*You know, Mommy, I'm going very far away,*
*farther than the sun and farther than the moon.*
*Where it never rains and never snows.*
*Where the sun always shines.  It's called Blue Tail, Mommy.*
*And Mommy, you can't come with me.*

I wondered at the time if Leslie's morning story was a reaction to the times I left her to go to work or to dinner or a movie with her father.  I wondered if she was inventing a place she could go to, to let me know how it felt to be left.  So, I made my face look very sad, mirroring what I saw on her face when I left her, hoping she would know I understood.  But I didn't understand at all.

Leslie began insisting on wearing yellow, only yellow.  She refused to buy new sneakers because we couldn't find yellow ones, and every day she wore her yellow slippers, her yellow dress, and her yellow hair ribbon to nursery school.  Yellow, like her silken hair.

Then, late one night, the journey began: The Angel of Death came for Leslie. It is said when this angel comes for children, she apologizes: "I am so sorry, I don't want to do this, but it is my job and I must."

The Angel of Death came very late one night, when I was awakened by the sound of Leslie sighing from her room:

*I go to her, sit down beside her and feel she has wet her bed. "Is that why you are sighing, Leslie? You silly. Let's just change your panties." I lift her legs to remove her wet pajamas. Her legs fall limp, the legs of a Raggedy Ann doll. Wave after wave of seizures are washing over her.*

Notice, please, that I tell you of those moments in the present tense because they will always be happening now, in this moment of telling. Such loss freezes time. Perhaps you know this to be true for your own loss, particularly if you have suffered a sudden and traumatic loss. Even if your loss happened long ago and far away, for loss knows no boundary of time. Perhaps like my loss, yours feels as if it happened only yesterday, is happening today. Now, as we sit in the garden, you may want to tell your story. You may want to write it in your journal, as I have written mine.

Leslie lay on the hospital bed in a coma for 10 days. I pleaded with the Angel of Death to let her stay, if only to live to smell a flower. On a rainy Sunday morning, Mother's Day, Leslie spread her wings and flew away. Her body lay on the bed, stilled, emptied—her spirit on the way to that place I could not go to with her, "Blue Tail."

*How does my daughter know? How do I not know? Perhaps she, so young, is still close to the thin veil separating the seen and unseen worlds. I don't know.*

What I do know is in Leslie's dying, her spirit took my hand and guided me across a dark threshold onto what felt like an impossible path of grief and into a journey that would last my lifetime.

When my daughter died, I began my unasked for and nexpected

initiation into a journey through grief.

I was more lost than I had ever been, with no compass to chart my way. Over the years, I have gained more insight, not only from my own personal experience of bereavement but also through helping others walk their own paths of grief. My daughter died in 1969, when I was 36 years old. Now, I am 83.

In 1975, I earned my Doctorate as a psychologist. Since then, I have worked with many people who have suffered loss. I believe my personal loss has taught me to travel the terrain of grief with others, like the blind who find their way by placing one foot in front of the other. On The Path of Grief, we, too learn to travel blind, step by step, one unimaginable day at a time. Through my own journey and journeying with others, I have learned to go slowly through that sorrow that is beyond words. I have learned to wait. To wait without hope until somehow, when it seems impossible to go on, an unexpected blessing arises to feed our stricken spirit in the vast desert of loss.

Looking back, I see my grief was not meant to be a burden I needed to "get over" or "move beyond."

This grief journey was to be my profound teacher, guiding me to embrace everything in this perilous and precious life—everything. Through my own pilgrimage in the country of Loss and Grief, I wrote this book in the hope it will serve as a comforting companion along the path of your journey.

## Suggestions For Using This Book

This book is for you to travel though if:
- your loved one is in the dying process, perhaps at home, perhaps in hospice care.
- your loved one has recently died, and you are in the rawness of

fresh grieving.

- if you are a young adult who has lost a parent or sibling and are in need

of a personal guide for your grief.

- you are in bereavement group, where you can share this book with others.

- you may be the facilitator of a bereavement group and can use this book as a guide.

- you are still dealing with the ongoing grief for the loss of some-one who died some time ago, perhaps

years and years ago.

- you have not yet lost anyone close to you, but you know Death will one day come and touch your life.

Please feel free to read through the entire book first, perhaps then returning to the beginning to contemplate each reflection, to sit with each guided meditation, to write from each journal suggestion.

Or you may prefer to open the book at random and linger with only those reflections, guided meditations, and journal writing sugges-tions that speak to you. Please know that there is no right or wrong way to use this book. It has emerged out of my own grief journey and hopefully you will find your own wise way to have it serve you.

## A Soul Space Of Solitude

We all need a place for the privacy of our self, where we can come to a stillness in which we hear our breathing, our inner voice, or simply sit in silence. As you journey through this book, consider pre-paring a quiet place in your home—a space that is yours to come to—where you can simply sit, reflect, meditate, write, or draw in your journal, where you can simply sit with yourself, being with each wave of your grief as it rises up into your awareness, waiting and wanting to be known by you.

Take the time to create a place of quiet in which you can come to take refuge. May it be a space where whatever arises within you can be invited to be present, to sit beside you, a place where you feel safe to be with your tears, smiles, fears, angers, hopes, regrets, and memories.

May this space of solitude become a haven for your grief.

May your grieving self have a physical refuge of its own, no matter how small.

May it be an uncluttered, comfortable space with some objects you treasure, or none at all.

May you come to cherish this space as your private place of solace.

May your simple, precious breath of life have space to be.

May every facet of your grief slowly find welcome in this place you have made for your grieving soul.

If some feelings are too painful to allow entry now, may they patiently stand and wait outside the door.

In time, may both your space of solitude and the space of your heart become a wide enough container of tenderness in which no feeling will be too much to bear, no matter how unbearable.

You may wish to begin and end your day in your soul space, sitting tenderly with whatever comes to you from within, listening to all that is, including feeling lost, for you are literally at a place called loss, far from life.

## *Reflections*

As you read the reflections along The Path of Grief, you will come to The Garden of Love and Loss to sit with others who have shared stories of their journey, many of whom I have sat with as a grief therapist.  As a companion along the way, I also share my own stories with you.  Together, we form a broken-hearted community, each finding our way to go on living with deepened love.

I offer 52 reflections, one per week for your first year of grief.  This first year is often a period of most painful mourning.  Of course, you can find this book of value if you come to it even long after the first year of your loss, even after many years.

Each reflection offers some seeds of understanding to sit with in the Garden of Loss and Love.  These seeds can be planted more deeply as you work with the guided meditations and journaling prompts.

## *Stories from Life*

Through the book, I will tell stories of the grief journey, stories from my life and from those of others.

It is healing to share our stories.  There will be invitations for you to tell yours in the journal writings.

## *Guided Meditations*

Meditation is a word that speaks for the many ways of creating awareness and entering inner space.  We can create our quiet, simple space, one that is physically comfortable and undistracted by the daily things that call to us.  You can turn the telephone off, put the computer to sleep, give yourself at least half an hour of time to simply be.

The tools of meditation available within this book are time-honored traditional practices:

• **Breath meditations:** The breath meditations will invite you to focus on your inhalation, your exhalation, and the resting breath in between.  In this focusing practice, you will find your breathing calming, your very nervous system slowing down. As your breath softens, becomes more flowing in its rhythm, you will find yourself more able to feel the feelings that arise from deep within you.

• **Somatic awareness of your body:** As you become aware of your breath, you are able to become aware of feelings that may be tightly held against grief. These feelings, which have been closed off from awareness to protect you from pain, wait in your body for you to receive them. The tools in this book may facilitate your ability to open and receive them with a tender heart.

• **Journal writing:** Writing even a single word that your grief utters can be a salve for your soul. One single word formed by your tears, by your lostness, by your stone-silence, holds a mirror to your grieving heart, helps you to be with your grief. In your journal, you can write your dreams, your precious memories, your regrets, and your hopes. Your journal is for you alone, and so you can write anything.

• **Drawing and movement:** Sometimes in your grief, when you do not have words, not even a single word, you may see a color that speaks for you. Your chosen color can move your feelings onto the blank page, thus bringing you to yourself. Or you may draw something that touches you from a dream or a memory with your loved one.

• **Guided meditations and movement:** Some of the guided meditations will invite you to move out of being frozen, shut down, depressed, or depleted in your grief. Even the smallest movement of a little finger allows the tiniest flow of life breath to stir and can express the deadness, sorrow, and loss wrapped in your grief. To see and feel the movement of your grief brings you the breath of your aliveness.

All of the reflections and guided meditations are meant to support you in being with your body, your feelings, and your spirit along this difficult path of grief.

You will see that many of the meditations ask you to enter the inner space of your imagination. The realm of imagination is a spiritual one and does not distinguish between time, before and after. Here, time is fluid and helps us flow between past, present, and future. When we open the doorway to imagination, we are able to be in any place at any time: past, present, and future. We are able to have contact with those who have died and gone on, even with our ancestors from long ago and far away, even with spiritual guides known and unknown, even with animal spirits. Imagination has no boundaries.

In imaginal space, we open ourselves to the vast life-giving possibilities of who and how we can be.

We can find it possible to repair hurts of the past that wait to be healed, forgive what seems unforgivable, and be touched by a solace we have not thought possible to ever receive again.

In entering guided mediation, know that what unfolds is shown the way by the deepest intentions of your heart.

Once I asked a rabbi, "What is intention?"

He replied: "Ah, intention—intention is everything! Let me give you an example: When a rabbi is getting ready to pray, he first sits quietly and prays that he should be able to pray."

As it is with us when we create a space to sit quietly, alone. We sit still for a moment, place our hand on our heart, and ask for what it is we deeply yearn for. Quietly, we listen, we hear.

You may not hear any words that utter the longing of your intention. Instead, you may sense something quietly opening within you, calling you to your true being. The Sufi tradition teaches that our heart's longing creates a vibration, called *himma*, which reaches an angel who stands on a bridge that crosses into the hidden world of imagination. The listening angel then responds to the himma of our heart by sending a dream, an image, something come as a surprise by touching us with new life.

In this time and space of imagination, the angel may send the smallest drop of beauty to touch your grief and nourish your spirit. Perhaps a tear will drop into the dry land of your grief. Feel the life of the tear drop. Hear its sound, hear its words, if any.

And, if the well of your heart is dry, bereft of even a single tear, let the desert of your grief be. Let your dry heart have the time and perhaps even the comfort of being known and sat with in your quiet space for as long as it takes for water to return to the well, even as it feels that the water of life shall never come again. The angel standing on the bridge will hear the longing of your dry heart when you cannot.

## *Journal Prompts*

There is nothing that cannot be written or drawn in your journal. No need to hide your words and images from yourself. I have found the greatest pain in my life comes from feelings I would not let myself feel, from words I would not let myself say, from tears I would not let myself cry. What I could not share with another, what I could barely share with myself, I shared with my journal.

During my long sojourn through the Land of Grief, I carried my journal wherever I went. My journal became a life raft to cling to when I felt lost at sea and terrified of drowning forever in grief. My journal and my sunglasses, to hide sudden unexpected tears, were my constant companions.

I recall one summer day. It was drizzling a soft, misty rain. I was walking slowly, aimlessly wandering through the park, holding Leslie's little blue umbrella over my head. I heard the raindrops falling on it.

Falling like tears. I did not think I could go on another step. I stopped under a tree and took out my journal and wrote:

> *I cannot bear the rain today pouring down*
> *while I walk under your little blue umbrella*
> *holding what I can of you*
> *I cannot bear the sun pouring warmth*
> *over me*
> *My arms ache to spread mother wings*
> *around you*
> *swoop you up, hold you*
> *to my breast*
> *My fingers cry to wipe the tears*
> *from your eyes*

My journals helped me find the words when they broke through my frozen feelings. To find words for unspeakable feelings is to discover who and where you are. The words are your tears being spoken.

Your tears are being rooted into some meaning, sprouting some sense out of the deadening senselessness of loss. As you hear yourself speak onto the page, as you later read what you have written, in those moments you find yourself. In those moments, you are anchored because you have spoken. For that moment at least, you are not lost in an unspeakable sea of sorrow, drowning in wordless tears or anger or numbness. Anything can be written in a journal. No one need read it but you.

As you write and draw, you will be gathering a record of your journey in the land of your grief. This will become a gathering of your journey that you may wish to revisit in the future and perhaps share with others close to you. Your journal will also map the places, inside and out, you have travelled along the way, the people and places and moments that have touched and brought healing. When I open one of the many journals on my shelf, I am amazed at what my ordinary mind has forgotten but what my body and spirit recall along my transformative grief journey.

You may forget about the places where you have stopped along The Path of Grief. But your journal will be a lasting source of healing recollection you can return to again and again as you make your way through the unfolding cycles of reflection and revelation.

When I look back into my journals, I see some pages have a single word written on them. In a dark hour, I wrote "light" with a yellow crayon and colored a yellow circle around it. I can see now it was a prayer, a plea for light to come into a darkness that felt endless, and this comforts still, even after all these years.

On your journal page, you can reach out to your loved one and write whatever words arise in your heart:

> *I shall always love you and miss you.*
> *I shall never forgive you for leaving me.*
> *It is hard not to hear you on the phone,*
> *not to walk with you,*
> *not to have breakfast on Sunday mornings, not to, not to,*
> *not to, not to...*

I also often wrote down quotations. Words written by fellow travelers struck a deep chord within, consoled and guided me, helped me sense someone beside me. I could hear and touch their words when I could not reach my own:

*There are parts of our hearts*
*whose existence we do not yet know*
*and suffering has to anchor them*
*to make us aware of their existence.*

—Le Bloy

Take your time to find the journal that is right for you, one that calls you, catches your eye, perhaps because of its color or pattern. Choose one with unlined pages so you may also draw if you wish. You will know it when you see it. Let your journal find you.

It will be helpful to have your journal beside you as you read each reflection, meditation, and journaling prompt. I also suggest that you have a set of colored pencils, crayons, or markers for drawing. Keep your journal and pencils at arm's reach in your private soul place. In my deepest grief, I always carried my journal with me. Even if I did not open it, I felt comforted by its presence.

Sometimes it felt urgent to simply write, "It hurts so much," to lift the pain from within me onto the page.

Sometimes I opened my journal and, without any words, moved a gray crayon along the page to give expression to the gray emptiness of the grief within and all around me. Sometimes you may want to write and, at other times, when there are no words, your hand may reach for the color that reflects your inner self at the moment and you may feel the inexplicable comfort of seeing something of your grief spread out on the open field in front of you.

# I.

# *Writing brings me comfort*

I F YOUR LOVED ONE IS STILL ALIVE, you may feel it is wrong to have feeling of grief while there is still life. Please know: There are no wrong feelings in this process of grief. You cannot prepare your grief as if from some recipe. You have your own emotional and spiritual rhythm to follow in dealing with your loss.

If your loved one has not yet died, or if your loved one has already died, your journal writing can become a consoling companion with whom you can share your tears, fears, and longings.

Your journal is a healing presence, always there for you, a witness to your feelings of grief. Your journal is for you alone, a conversation between you and your heart to be shared only when and with whom you wish, or perhaps never to be shared. Your journal gives you a space for the privacy of your deep self.

You may feel overwhelmed by tending to the one who is dying. You may feel there is no room for you, for your feelings, for your tears. However, it is important to make room for yourself, so you will have the strength to take care of your loved one. You, the caretaker, need compassionate care so that you do not become depleted and unable to give of yourself, physically, emotionally, and spiritually.

Let yourself be aware of where you are along the path of grieving for the person who is leaving you or has already left. See where you are standing now, at this crossroad in your life. Give yourself the time and the presence to know what you need.

Reflect upon what you want to remember from this time.

Writing down a sentence or two can be powerful. I recall, when my father was dying, I sat quietly beside him in his wheelchair and in the quiet, deep within, I heard, "Judith, what do you want this precious fleeting time with your dad to be?" Later, I wrote in my journal,

*May we sit quietly together.*

*May each of us take in the deep and healing and hard-earned love that will abide forever.*

*May we each be grateful for this precious, fleeting time together.*

And we were.

What you write in these crucial days will sustain you in the days to come—the solace of recognizing, hearing, and writing your feelings, all of them.

There may be things you can't bring yourself to say to your loved one face-to-face right now. Your feelings will wait for their words to be spoken into your journal, or up into the open heavens, or shared with someone. You can speak your feelings by writing in your journal or saying them to a friend. What is important is that you give yourself permission to find the words to express your feelings, so they do not fall into an abyss of the "never to be spoken." Feelings and words sealed behind walls become deadened and deaden us.

Finding words for your feelings can bring healing on the dark path of your grief. Words, perhaps the words of a song that soothes you, or a prayer, or perhaps one single word you find yourself breathing, will be there for you to lean on as you go on. Perhaps even the simplest words, such as "Please, send a word to help me."

## Guided Meditation: Prayer Seeds

TO BEGIN, SIT QUIETLY *with your journal and colored pencils. Turn to the first blank page. Open the box of pencils. Take out the color you are most drawn to. Take this pencil and place it beside your book.*

*Now, close your eyes. Slowly start to breathe in... and out . . .in. . .and out. . .*

*See your hands relaxing and quietly coming together to form a cup.*

*Sit with your cupped hands, let them open toward the heavens.*

*As you sit quietly in this way, sense how the invisible heavens are breathing one word into the cup of your hands.*

*Listen carefully until you hear the word that appears.*

*Let your mouth utter the word sent to you, aloud or in a whisper.*

*Let your hands rest open on your lap, open to receive the one word.*

*Let this one word drop into your breathing, whispering through your body as you breathe.*

*Know how this one word, dropped down deep into your heart, will go on being breathed through every organ and cell of your being, even as you stop noticing it.*

*Sense how this word brings you tender healing and prepares you for your next breath, for your next step through grief.*

*You may find it comforting to sit for 10 minutes or more, breathing your word or words, in and out.*

*You may find your breath and the sound of your word becoming one, flowing through your heart and every organ of your body and through the river of your bloodstream.*

*You may choose to whisper this one word as your breathing softens and you close your eyes to drift off to sleep. When you awake in the morning, you may hear this one seed prayer on your breath as you open your eyes. Breathe it in. Breathe it out.*

*You will know when it is time to be quiet again, to cup your hands to the heavens, and listen within and to receive another word, another healing prayer seed to grow within you as you journey through grief.*

## *In your journal*

WHEN YOU ARE READY, write your word or words in the center of a page of your journal.

Circle it in with the color that calls to you.

As you write this word seed, be sure to slowly breathe in and breathe out.

As you begin slowly writing, know you are planting this word deep into your whole self, where it will grow silently in the soil of your being, bringing healing into your life.

Remember, your journal is there for you at any time of day or night.

You do not need to write much. A word. A sentence.

A fleeting moment that opens to you: perhaps you and your loved one looking at one another with a never-to-be-forgotten expression of openheartedness.

Give yourself the space of solitude. Hear what wants to move from your heart to your pen to the page of your journal. Write with your tears, your sorrow, your anger, and let every part of you write itself onto the page.

# 2.

# *I begin to grieve*

IN THE BEGINNING, YOU TRY EVERYTHING. You exhaust every possibility. You search for any doctor who might help. You look for
the healer, the tre is wrong; this isn't happening; you will wake up
from this nightmare. You hope against hope because you have no
choice, for this is the nature of love: Love is the hope you hold in your
heart. We are hard-wired to hope, to protect our loved ones from
harm, to move mountains, to defeat death.

There is a natural human refusal, an incomprehension stopping us
from accepting the reality of death.

Death is too final, too stark for us to take in. Your loved one may
well be experiencing the same struggle, for denying death serves a purpose: It is our protection against the unimaginable, the unthinkable.
Like the need for sunglasses to protect us from the direct glare of a
blinding sun, we cannot stare straight into the face of death's reality
without staggering, without being blinded.

You may find you are slowly letting the reality of death sink in, while at the same time continuing to deny it. The curtain of the denial of death lifts and falls, again and again. Our struggle in coming to terms with the reality of death, with life's impermanence, becomes a slow, on-going process. You see the truth: Death is coming or has already come, but you dare not give up trying to control this reality.

You refuse to accept that you have no control over this ultimate of leavings. Isn't love strong enough to move mountains? If you just try harder to do something, surely you can stop or maybe delay death from coming!

But there comes a time, after waging a valiant fight for life, when you know everything that could be done has been done. When the doorway of acceptance begins to open, you feel powerless and defeated and so very weary from the long battle. You feel you should have done more. You feel there is nothing more you can or could do. Perhaps you are depressed because you feel you have failed. Perhaps, even so, you know deep in your heart that you have loved well and done your best. The truth is we are all mostly good husbands, wives, partners, sons, daughters, mothers, fathers, siblings, or friends. You know you did all that was humanly possible but feel you have reached the limits of your powers to control life and death and must somehow accept this reality. Accepting death into our lives is a difficult task that is not supported or promoted by our culture, which teaches us to deny death, to try to defeat it.

Yet here, in this time of facing the end with your loved one, you are brought to a threshold of meeting death on intimate terms as an abiding part of your life, of all life.

It is important to understand what has happened to you in the last months, weeks, and days you have spent with your loved one. These days may have had the precious ring of the everyday, the ordinary you have come to treasure, knowing its impermanence. As you sat together, ate together, walked together, laughed and cried together, you may have come to understand you were standing at a threshold, holding death in one hand and the sacredness of everyday life in the other, living suspended between the ongoing flow of life and the razor-edge awareness of death. Boundaries between life and death—once so distinct—begin to collapse. Death, usually on the outskirts of your geography, now sits at the center of your life, disorienting you from your known world. The shifting sands of life and death may literally make you dizzy, suddenly confused as to where you stand on the borderland of life turning toward death.

As the time approaches for your loved one to cross the threshold, you who stand closest to that gateway also face a profound transition. You stand beside someone who is meeting the limitations of the power of their will. You have witnessed his attempts to defeat death. You may have watched her mortification as every heroic medical attempt has failed. You have lived with the daily weakening of his physical body. You have been present as you and your loved moved through the rhythms of courage, rage, and despair and opened to a deep sadness beyond protest into acceptance of what is to come.

You, along with the one who is dying, are experiencing the faltering of your sense that life holds together in the ways you always thought it would. As you hold the hand of the dying one, you are led to an unimaginable threshold. Once at that threshold where you must release your loved one to cross over without you, you may find yourself standing dazed on the edge of this reality, not totally in life, not totally in death, but somewhere in between. You have seen death coming, have seen it arrive. You will see body and spirit here and then not here. You will witness what is left behind, the body an emptied cocoon, the butterfly of spirit flown away, and yourself—not knowing how you will go on yet knowing somewhere in your depths that somehow you will.

Inevitably, when you stand on the edge where things are present and then disappear, where there is something and then, suddenly, nothing, where there once was the breath of life, and now, only silence and emptied space, you will falter. The vessel that holds and illumines your sense of solid reality in now broken, the shattered pieces fallen into a void beyond human knowing. As your loved one crosses over into death, you can follow only so far, for it is not your time to go into that unknown place. It is your time to remain here and begin your own profound crossing from the threshold of death back onto the journey that is yours, into the land of your grief.

## *Guided Meditation: The Gate of Life and Death*

*MAKE YOURSELF PHYSICALLY COMFORTABLE in your quiet place.*

*Loosen any tight clothing. Feel your body well supported as you sit or lie down.*

*Come to your breathing, allow the whole soft front of you to rise and fall.*

*If there are waves of tears, let them wash through you. Give them their space and time.*

*If your chest is tight with holding back tears, gently place a hand on your chest.*

*Allow the tightness to breathe as it is—no pressure, no forcing, just a tender hand.*

*Upon your heart space, feel the movement of your breath.*

*Close your eyes and allow your awareness to turn inward.*

*Come to the space of your imagination where anything is possible.*

*As you breathe, let your exhalation become long, see your*

*out breath, or exhale, become a path.*

*See yourself walking on this path, sense your feet touching the ground you are walking on.*

*Be aware of all you see and sense around you.*

*Become aware of your loved one beside you, present either in body or spirit.*

*Walk together until you reach a beautiful gate.*

*Know it to be the Gate of Life and Death.*

*Know this is as far as you can go with your loved one.*

*Standing at the gate, see it slowly open.*

*See a gentle spirit reaching out with open, loving arms.*

*See its hands gently take hold of the hands of your loved one—in body, if still alive; in spirit, if already dead.*

*Or, perhaps, you see yourself lifting up the body and spirit of the one who is dying or has died into the hands of the one who waits to receive and guide your loved to the other side of the Gate of Life and Death.*

*See what this spirit looks like: perhaps an angel, a beloved family member already on the other side of the Gate of Life and Death, or an ancestor or spirit guide.*

*Whoever it may be, sense and feel how your loved one is crossing over to the other side of life, being helped by the care of a most compassionate and wise being who has already crossed over.*

*Stand at the gate.*

*See your loved one go on, slowly fading into a holy light. Feel and sense this light.*

*Now, stand and breathe as you see the gates slowly close.*

*Sense and feel if anything remains that wants to happen. Take your time.*

*See your loved one being led away from you into a mystery, beyond anything you can possibly know, as you stand on this side of the Gate of Life and Death.*

*Be with your feelings. Sense your body. Be with all you feel, sense, and understand.*

*Now, slowly, with awareness, turn from the Gate toward the path on which you came to this spot.*

*See yourself returning to life that waits for you here.*

*Know you have given and have been the best of yourself and have gone as far on the journey with your loved one as was possible for you.*

*Take some time to be with all that sits within you now.*

## *In your journal*

YOU MAY WANT TO WRITE your journey as a story, from beginning to end.

Accompanying your departed one to pass through the Gate of Life and Death is a sacred time. You may be able revisit that time now in a way you could not at the actual time of death. Perhaps Death came suddenly. Perhaps you were not there beside your loved one when he or she left. Perhaps your loved one's dying was traumatic, and you are still absorbing and unwinding it.

Now, in your meditation and in your journal, you can have the slow time, the solitude, and the solace of your soul space. Now, you can take your time.

As you write your experience, let yourself go slowly, take time to close your eyes, to see and sense all that is happening for you now in this space of slow awareness.

Be in touch with any sense of healing that is happening for you and your loved one as you take leave of one another at the Gate of Life and Death.

Anything that sits in your heart to be spoken, to be felt, to be received can happen now.

Take your time. Let all that wants to be open into this space of writing.

# 3.

## *Making peace*

WHAT DOES IT MEAN FOR YOU to be losing or to have lost this person in your life, to have the threads of this precious one unwinding from your life? Is it a father, a mother, a husband, a wife, a child, a brother, a sister, or a dear friend you are losing? Wrapped into these words are the many intimate meanings contained in your deep relationship. We don't fully know what our relationships mean to us until we see our loved one leaving and then gone, until we sense the vulnerability of our being left at a place called loss. The empty spaces that are left somehow reveal how much this loved one gave to our life.

When they were alive, there were fine threads, vibrating filaments, energetic cords that went between your heart and theirs, your stomach and theirs, your mind and theirs. Now, those cords of connection may continue vibrating, still holding the connections, as they slowly unwind and become fainter and fade. You may feel them as both sacred and achingly painful. In your missing, you may be called to your body, where you sense the pulsating life that once connected you. You may listen and find yourself meditating on the qualities of your relationship that remain living in your body.

You may find the feelings connected to the one you are losing are not always positive. This reality may feel disturbing to you if you believe at this time of dying you should be all-loving, all-caring. But relationships are no different before, during, or after death. Relationships go on and on being complex, challenging us to grow and find ways to repair, and teaching us how to love. Only now, with Death nearing, there is so little time to face the flaws that call out for compassionate healing.

Allow yourself to know your hurts, angers, and judgments as they sit in the privacy of your self. Be with them in your space of solitude. If you use your energy to suppress your feelings, you are likely to suppress your loving feelings as well. Your relationship is a richly woven and complicated tapestry. If you are true and honest with yourself, you will see how, unless you are a saint, you carry a wide array of feelings for the ones you are close to.

In letting all of your less-than-loving feelings sit at the table with you, you make room for the fullness of loving feelings to sit there as well, so all of you can be present, and you can be fully human. To allow ourselves to be fully human is to allow all of our feelings, without labels of "good" or "bad," or "positive" or "negative." Without the labels, your feelings have a quality of "suchness," of just being alive in how they are now, no different than an animal whose feelings arise into its innocent body, moving through and releasing. If our feelings are swept under the carpet, we may believe we have banished them, but, in reality, they find their way—an expression on a face; a turn of the word; a sudden, unexpected eruption of anger. Better to welcome all of our feelings into non-judging awareness, to hold them in tenderness so. Then, we are likely more able to accept the full spectrum of the feelings toward the one who is dying or has died.

In sitting with the full spectrum of your feelings, without condemning them or exiling them as "not good," you may find your heart soften for both yourself and your loved one. You may release both of you from the stories of blame and reach down into regrets for what could not or will not be. You may touch onto your true needs that were not met in your relationship, or your loved one's needs that you could not meet. In allowing the full palette of your feelings, you are also conveying with your energy that the one who is dying may feel their feelings as well. In this way, you clear your relationship of the weight of unfinished business.

Being in touch with your difficult feelings may help you reflect on all that is dear in this one. If your loved one is still alive, you may look deeply and softy into his or her eyes and express with your eyes—or words— what you are already beginning to miss. If there is still time to allow the vulnerability of love and awareness of loss to be revealed and shared with mutual gratitude, with words, touch, or looks, know how sacred this time is for both of you and how it will remain treasured in your memory.

Even if you do not speak your feelings aloud, if you feel them and let them move through your body, held with acceptance, your loved one will sense a release, a softening of your being. As you accept your feelings, you can be more present, less bound up in keeping your feelings hidden from yourself and the other. What may count even more than the spoken words between the two of you is your presence, the music of the softened, open, honest heart that accepts all that is and can be seen upon your face.

## Guided meditation: Sorting threads of connection

SIT QUIETLY . . . close your eyes . . . come to your breathing.
As you breathe, see yourself across from the one who is in

*the process of dying.*

*If the person has already died, enter the space of imagination, and see the person standing across from you or reclining in a bed or chair.*

*Be aware of how there are threads of connection passing between the two of you.*

*Some are threads that move from heart to heart, others from belly to belly, or from hand to hand.*

*As you breathe, be aware of the connecting cords of energy moving back and forth between the two of you, threads of loving and also those that are less than loving.*

*As you breathe, be aware of the threads that are wound with painful parts of your relationship that wait to be unwound with the healing of letting go, of letting be, of forgiveness.*

*Disappointment in whatever promise this relationship has not fulfilled.*

*Exhaustion, both emotional and physical, because this person's illness has wearied you.*

*Anger for the burdens he or she leaves behind for you to tend.*

*And guilt for your anger.*

*Regret for feeling you could not live up expectations, to be the caretaker you had hoped to be, or for things that could not be healed before Death came.*

*Allow the painful threads between you to unwind and fall into a golden circle that you see on the ground beside you.*

*See if there are any other threads that wait to be unwound between the two of you.*

*Notice if there remains a most difficult thread, one most painful, one you least want to see, know, and feel.*

*Allow these last, stubborn threads to unwind and find their place in the golden circle on the ground before you.*

*When you have placed the last thread into the golden circle, allow yourself to feel what it is like to free one another from carrying unfinished business.*

*And then, see all the threads you have released into the golden circle carried away by a gentle breeze, beyond where you can see, far away into the heavens, where they dissolve into pure, golden light.*

*Be still and feel the relief of letting go. Breathe relief in and then out.*

*Now, see how there is a single thread of connection that remains, still pulsing between the two of you, from heart to heart. Sense this to be the thread of the undying cherishing of the life you have shared.*

*Know how, although you must now let go of the physical life of your loved one, the thread of connection remains, never to be lost. See the color of this thread. See what it is made of. Feel where it is carried in your body. Know how it keeps you in eternal connection with your loved one.*

*Let yourself feel how threads of grief are also a part of what you carry, intertwined with the thread of lasting love.*

*Know and feel the richness and realness of all that you carry, the broken, the tattered, and the whole—the entire weaving of your relationship.*

*Allow yourself to acknowledge that some relationships are more complicated than others. Now or in days to come, you may discover threads of unfinished business that remain unwound. It is possible that you may not be able to unwind some threads, perhaps not now, perhaps not ever. To know this is also part of coming to a certain acceptance of our losses and with the limits of our capacity to make things perfect or "right."*

*As you sit and breathe in your quiet space, give yourself the solace of knowing you will go on working through your relationship until you come to a place of forgiveness and acceptance, even if this cannot be accomplished until long after the person is gone.*

*Or perhaps it never will. May you come, then, to hold the complex threads of this relationship with a tender heart. And may you find within your being the indestructible thread at the heart of your relationship.*

*Accept the reality that some of your relationships, perhaps even one most important to you, will sit at the center of your being and stir a certain kind of poignant knowing that you have done the best you can.*

## *In your journal*

DRAW THOSE THREADS OF DARK FEELINGS that wait to be unwound from your relationship.

Choose the colors. Name each feeling, each thread. Breathe as you draw.

As you exhale, be with letting go, releasing what no longer wants or needs to be carried by you.

Taking your time, draw the most difficult thread or threads to be released and name them.

Write what may want to be spoken for each thread.

Sense and feel how you are completing unfinished business.

You may want to take these threads and, instead of releasing them, reweave the colors to express the complexity of your relationship. If so, take each dark and light thread and, with colors you choose, draw a weaving on the page to reflect the intricate pattern of your connection with the one who has already departed or will depart.

If there are threads you are ready to release, draw these threads, name them, and draw a golden circle around them. Then draw the breeze carrying them away.

If you are not ready to release these difficult threads, know there will be time to do so as you move along your journey and find your way.

Lastly, draw the golden circle, empty of all you have released.

From out of your quiet center, draw the thread that remains and is indestructible in the center of the circle.

Feel and know how your tender heart is like this circle, holding the abiding thread of love at its core.

# 4.

## *I let my love be known*

AS ADULTS, WE OFTEN HESITATE to be completely open with our love, fearing we'll receive a less-than-loving response in return. We feel safer expressing ourselves freely with children because they tend to be so generously open with their love. They run toward us eagerly, lift up open faces full of trust, expecting to be showered with our love and acceptance. We can easily meet children's trust with our own spontaneity. But because we know adults can be less open, less secure, and more guarded, we tend to stay in our safe zone and withhold expressions of love. We too often wait to express our love, we wait for special occasions, put if off till tomorrow, wait for others to "go first."

But now there can be no waiting; you are with someone whose tomorrows are numbered. In times of life and death, tomorrow is clearly revealed to be the illusion it is. No one knows for certain what time has in store for us, what tomorrow will bring, what will happen in the next moment. When you are close to someone who is ill or dying, tomorrow is meaningless. My daughter Leslie was healthy when she went to bed one night and in a coma before the light of next day. You, too, may know how today, this moment, this time together, is all there is. It is all we have, and it is a precious gift of this one more moment of life. Now, right now is a gift to be cherished. It takes loss to show us that this is not a platitude but the deepest depth of reality. This moment. This moment.

Your loved one may be connected to wiring and tubes, may be ravaged by pain, may not even look like the person you love. He or she may be irritable, angry, or wrapped in despair. You may feel there is no room in this painful and frightening atmosphere for the expression of your love. You may not even be aware of your love because so many medical and emotional barriers stand between you and your loved one and between you and your own heart. Your heart may feel frozen with the shock of loss. You may feel the stress of making sure the nurses and doctors are doing their best. You may feel angry at waiting for help to come when it's needed. There may be no opening you can even imagine for your heart to have a place.

Just as in life, so in the face of death, a myriad of blocks stops us from expressing our love. Your true feelings and good intentions may be blocked by fear of the changed person you see before you, by anger that she is leaving you to face life alone. Or you may feel you need to hide your emotions, hide your fear and grief behind a mask of strength to assure him and yourself that he is not causing you to suffer, to show him and yourself how you are standing strong.

Whatever blocks the expression of your love, know that your loved one is likely facing similar barriers and may feel just as isolated. Perhaps each of you is feeling a similar longing for connection before it is too late. Perhaps you both hunger to look into each other's eyes, to show your love, reveal your need, and share your fear and sadness to be losing one another.

When you find your way to reach out with soft, honest eyes, you may touch tenderly and perhaps even reawaken passion and compassion before death comes.

## *Guided meditation: Opening the door to my heart's love*

SIT QUIETLY IN YOUR PLACE OF SOLITUDE. *Close your eyes. Come to your breathing.*

*Allow your awareness to turn inward.*

*Ask, how can I open the door to let my love come out and reveal itself?*

*Breathe in and out as you listen for the answer that comes.*

*Feel where this door sits in your body . . . sense any tightness, any heaviness.*

*Perhaps the door closing off your love sits as tightness in your stomach, your solar plexus, or your throat.*

*Take all the time you need to slowly scan your body and find where the tightening of your loving lives.*

*Place your hand on the part of your body where the tightness sits and look inside.*

*What do you see? What do you touch? How does it feel? Stay with any sensations that come.*

*Name what you sense and feel.*

*Now, look beneath the tightness you find in your body, beyond the door closing your love away.*

*Be aware of how your love wants to show itself in these very last, precious days you share with your loved one.*

*Breathe softly as you find your love sitting in a clear and quiet place in the very center of your heart, waiting for you.*

*Let your love move through your heart.*

*See and sense your face as the face of love, your eyes as the eyes of love, your voice as the voice of love.*

*Know and feel the strength of tenderness that is yours as you allow your love to move through you.*

*Now, take a long breath and see your loved one in front of you, either physically or in your meditation.*

*Look into the center of the heart of your loved one.*

*See his love, perhaps hidden like yours and pulsating at the very core of him.*

*See how her love is unchanged by any changes in her mind or body.*

*See how his core of love is unchanged by the effects of illness, pain, medical procedures, or medications.*

*Know that not even the deep sleep of coma can erase this love: It is always there, abiding in the deep center of our being.*

*Let the core of love in you speak to the core of love in the other.*

*Hear what your core of love says. Perhaps it speaks with a sound, a gesture, a ray of light, or with tears, touch, or a quiet smile.*

*Wait and listen to what the core of love in your loved one says to you.*

*Listen. Be still. Feel how abiding this love is. Know how it wants to express itself.*

*You may be sitting quietly together as your core of love begins to speak, "You know how much I love you. If you do not know, I let you know now. I will miss you terribly. I know you are going, but I'll never stop loving you." You may speak aloud or silently.*

*Your core of love may share tears, or you may touch,*

*quietly holding hands.*

*You may listen to music together or be held in sacred silence.*

*You may look into his eyes. Comb her hair. Bathe his feet. Bring a single rose.*

*Make love for the last time.*

*You need only listen to your heart to know what your love wants to reveal.*

*As you listen, tears may come. Let them for they are part of your love.*

*In the precious time you have left, know that in your quietness you can hear your love and sense the ways it longs to be free, to make itself known, to give and receive the great gift of never-ending love.*

## *In your journal*

GIVE YOURSELF THE TIME IN YOUR QUIET SPACE to sit with this reflection and meditation.

Keep your journal open at your side and your pencils available.

Follow through the meditation and allow your breath and feelings to move.

When you reach the core of your love, write from there to your loved one Write for 10 minutes without stopping.

Let what wants to come from your heart flow on to the page.

Do not stop writing, do not edit, allow your love to do the writing.

Write what may block your love, allow the block.

Know how the more you allow the block to open, to speak onto the page, you are allowing the flow of your core love to open.

Do this for the sake of Love, for your love, and for the love of the one who is dying or has already died.

# 5.

# *I let my loved one know they can leave me and be at peace*

NINA WAS MY FRIEND FOR OVER 30 YEARS, *one of the friends I call sister-friend. Nina began to weaken after a year-long struggle with cancer. She was bedridden at home and exhausted, and her friends could see she was losing her valiant struggle.*

*But Nina would not let go. We understood: She had just turned 50, was vibrant with Christmas light eyes, was filled with love and talents to give to life. Though her time to leave was approaching, she never spoke of dying. Perhaps Nina thought about leaving us, but it was an unspoken secret, although not a well-hidden one.*

*Nina's young son Jesse had struggled in school and Nina rallied her energies to make sure he was settled in an appropriate high school before allowing herself to become bedridden. Nina had ongoing concerns about Jesse, so she forced life to go on as usual, held Death at bay, willed her body to recover so she could take care of her son. Everyone but Nina could see she was not going to recover. But Nina continued to cling to life, and we, her friends, remained loyal at her side and watched her struggle.*

*When I arrived for my morning visit one day, Jesse was sitting on the edge of Nina's bed. As I sat beside her bed she turned to me and said, "Last night, in the middle of the night, I called Jesse. He came to sit by my bed and told me how he felt. He said, 'Mom, it's getting too difficult for both of us. It's okay if you die.'" Later that morning, friends arrived and we all sat around Nina's bed, under her open window. As the birds sang their sweet songs of life, we let Nina go. Two hours later, she had flown away.*

*During the nights that followed, meditating upon the loss of my beloved friend, I found myself lighting a candle. I sensed Nina still needed reassurance that it was all right to let go, to be at rest. I talked to her spirit. I told her, "Be at peace. Your children will be loved, well cared for, and safe. They will have a home and all the security they need. You have done your best for them. Now, be at peace."*

People who are dying often hold on. They cling to life and to their loved ones just as we hold on to them. No loving person wishes to separate from their loved ones, especially when they are needed, when they feel their children need them. Part of the responsibility we have toward our loved ones is to face our need to hold them close. Sometimes you cannot bear to let go because you think you will have failed to heal them with your love. Sometimes you feel you can't go on living without your loved one and this sends them a strong message to hold on to their life for your sake. And so, for the sake of the one who is dying, and for the sake of our own journey, we do our own hard grief work of releasing our loved one. This means facing our need to hold them to us, not being able to bear letting them go.

*Susan, who is 70 years old, tells me with a quivering voice, "I won't let go. I've been married to him for 50 years. I don't know how to live without him. I'm not ready to die and I can't live alone. He can't leave me yet." Then, deep tears come. Shortly after her tears of release, Susan and I sit quietly together. On her face, I can see her anguish turning to a deep sadness of accepting reality. Susan returns to the hospital, approaches her husband's hospital bed, takes both his hands in hers, and says, "Sam, you have been a good husband to me. I love you. I don't want you to suffer anymore. It will be hard for me, but I will keep your strength as a part of me. I love you and I let you go. I promise you, I will go on." Softly, after months of suffering, Sam holds Susan's hands and peacefully slips away.*

Maybe you simply cannot tell your loved one that you are ready to let them go. Perhaps it is too much for you to bear. Perhaps your loved one is not able to accept the reality of Death coming. And yet you both know deep in your heart that the time is near. Even if you cannot say the words, your eyes can see and speak. Your tender touch can speak. Your love can speak, even without words. "I see how you are suffering. I love you. I can barely let go of holding you here. And yet, for your peace, I ease my holding of you. I release you with love into the Great Love."

Even if your loved one died before you were able tell them you were ready to let them go, you can still speak to them, just as I spoke to Nina after she had gone. You can speak to your loved one's spirit, let them know all will be well between you and assure them you will be all right and will find your way.

That it will not be easy, but you will go on. For the sake of not holding them here, give them the blessing that they can rest in peace. And, as you go on alone after their death, you can continue to talk to your loved one, say what is in your heart, finally find the words and speak them to their spirit.

## *Guided meditation: Holding on, letting go*

SIT QUIETLY, RELAX INTO YOUR BREATHING, *and whisper to your body, "Be at ease. Be at ease."*

*Whisper to your shoulders, face, neck, arms, hands and fingers, chest and belly, to your jaw and tongue, "Rest now, breathe, be at ease."*

*Move your awareness through your body, allowing the tight places to soften, whispering, "Be at ease. Be at ease"*

*Feel your body slowly unwinding. No forcing. Only gently guiding each body part, each muscle, to relax.*

*Where you feel a tightness, know this as a place where you may be holding tight to your loved one because you are not ready to live without their physical presence.*

*Breathe into the tightness, feel it, let the holding on be there, let it tighten more and more.*

*Feeling this tightness, know how you are trying to hold your loved one to you with the sheer force of your will, for dear life.*

*Feel the firm grip your body has on what you cannot yet bear to release.*

*Without judgment, simply be present with this holding.*

*You can speak to this holding place in yourself, sit with it, and hold an inner conversation of your struggle to both let go and hold on.*

*Breathe, allow your feelings. "It is true, I am holding on and I will not, I cannot let go of you, not now, not ever."*

*You may become aware of feelings of terror, of aching emptiness, of a hole inside you and in the world, as you anticipate or already sit in your loss.*

*You may find your hand reaching to touch a place of tight-*

*ness in your body.*

*You may find tears welling, as this place in your body knows it is being seen and accepted. Let the tears and emotions flow.*

*Your feelings are real and true and, as much as it hurts, it is life-giving to allow their movement.*

*If there is a trembling, let it move through.*

*Know how you are like the innocent animal, whose body trembles, for as long as it takes for the waves of feeling to move through.*

*Perhaps you are readying to tell your loved one that, no matter how hard, you will find a way to accept the coming of Death.*

*You may say to your loved one, face to face or in the space of your meditation, "I am slowly releasing you. It is so very hard. I do it for your sake so that you can go in peace and rest in peace. Be at peace now. Let go. You are loved now and forever. And I do it for me. I release you and I can carry you in my heart and go on in this life. You will always live in me and guide my way."*

*Allowing your feelings, you may sense a loosening, a letting be of what is true within you.*

*Let yourself feel the unwinding that comes from giving presence to your strong feelings of holding on.*

*Sense golden pulsing cords of connection between your loved one and yourself, from heart to heart.*

*Sense them, always present, eternal, and know how your softening, your holding on, allows these golden cords to breathe.*

*As you allow the tight grip on your feelings to begin to*

*loosen, your loved one will feel a shift in you, sense the energy of your intention when they look into your eyes, and feel grateful for your tender spoken or unspoken blessings to release them into a peace and love beyond this life.*

*Before going to be with your loved one or upon returning, you may find support in coming to your quiet space, to be with this meditation, to unwind your tight places, to let the difficult feelings and words open, to feel gratitude for the courage of your heart to feel, sense, and utter the difficult letting go.*

## *In your journal*

OPEN TWO CLEAR FACING PAGES.

Sit quietly and allow your breath to take you to the place in your body that holds tightly, fearing, refusing to release your loved one.

Don't try to change this sense in your body. Let the tight holding on be.

On one page, draw this tightness. Listen to it speak. Write what it says.

Now, if you are ready, find in your body, even if it is a very small place, the felt sense of letting go, of releasing your loved one.

Draw this letting go. Listen to it speak. Write its words.

In quiet meditation, let yourself move back and forth from the tight holding place in your body and on the page to the releasing place of your body and on the page.

Let yourself know that both are places for you to bring your tender heart to, one neither one better than the other. Just flowing feelings, wanting to be heard, honored, and written about.

Notice if the feelings shift at all as you sit with them, give them your presence, and let them speak onto the page.

If you cannot imagine coming to letting go, let feelings of holding on just be. Let them be. It may help to write the words that come in your journal. Writing what you cannot say face-to-face—and barely to yourself—helps you speak your truth and eases the held places in your body. This movement of unwinding energy will help your loved one know they, too, can release their holding. Even without words, the unwinding will be a tender music between the two of you.

# 6.

# *I form intentions*

I N THE MONTHS FOLLOWING THE DEATH *by suicide of my dear brother-friend Jules, I found myself filling an old earthenware vase each morning with fresh spring flowers to sit on the sunlit windowsill in my kitchen. One day, as I meditatively placed each spring flower into the vase, I wondered: What are you doing Judith, as you linger, as you search for the place for each flower in this simple earthenware vase?*

*What was my heart's desire, my intention, in those quiet morning moments of my flower meditation? I listened, and I heard the answer to my question: You are expressing your desire to carry on the sacred beauty of your friend's life before his heart broke beyond repair. The Light of an inner divine flame was moving me to form a loving gesture toward the spirit of my dear friend. I wept tender tears as I recalled our walks through the meadows at Point Reyes, where the beautiful wild flowers bloomed.*

Intention is your deepest desire to be able to offer to life what sits at the center of your heart, to express who you truly are in your pure aliveness. There are times you come to know your intention only by noticing the movement of a spontaneous gesture you see yourself expressing, like my gesture of lifting each flower toward the old vase. When you are moved from deep within to act or to speak your truth, to do something that you feel called to do and must say "yes" to: that is your intention welling up from your depths. Intention is your wish to express your heart's deepest desire and aliveness, asking you to carry it forth, not to silence it.

In your grief, you have already expressed many intentions, difficult at times, some you may have thought impossible: to have the strength to bear the fullness of your grief, to give voice to your sadness, to uncover the essence of what your loved one means to you, and carry it on into life, to let your loved one know you will find your way when he or she leaves you.

We cannot act upon intentions by rote, simply for the sake of fulfilling an obligation. There is a difference between fulfilling an obligation and being moved by our intention. To be life-giving, our intentions need to come from our heart. Our true intentions rise out of our vulnerable places where our sacred needs abide. They cannot be mandated by rules or conventions. When we feel our intentions rise from deep in our bodies and form words upon our lips, they will guide us to express and live our deepest truth.

Your intention means everything. With it, you focus your consciousness toward expressing your heart's desire to sanctify life. The intentions of your heart will give you strength and dignity to prevail and to gather the sparks of light that have scattered from your shattered, grieving soul. Living our intention can be very simple, like meditating on wildflowers as they are placed into the vase. Or our intention can, for example, be a large commitment to the life of the environment, to fulfill a deeply shared commitment with the one who has passed.

Particularly in the face of death, we are called to live from the bare bones of who we are, for there will be no other time when we can live these moments with this one in any other way, on any other day.

Like the phoenix singing a prayerful song before it rises up through the flames to be reborn, our intention to go through the darkness of grief, through the brokenness and barren silence, is what enables us to rise, in time, into renewed wholeness and unfold into new life.

If you cannot gather your intention just yet, that, too, is all right. On the path of your grief, everything will come in its time. Perhaps, like the rabbi who went into a small room to pray that he should be able to pray, you, too, shall, in the silence of your soul, ask to one day be able to live once again in your heart's deepest longing.

## Guided meditation: Listening to my heart's intention

TAKE THE TIME TO SIT QUIETLY IN YOUR PRIVATE PLACE.

Close your eyes and come to your breathing. Breathe in. Breathe out.

Be aware of the still place of pause after each exhalation of your breath as you wait for the next inhalation.

Sense this space between your breaths as a very quiet, restful space.

When it is time, be aware of the next inhalation as it comes to you.

You do not have to do anything for your breath to come and go.

Allow your breath to move in its own rhythm.

*Let yourself be breathed.*

*As you breathe in this way, notice both your outer and inner space becoming more and more quiet.*

*Feel and sense how, as you sit with awareness of you breathing, you let go of your obligations in outer time.*

*As you sit simply breathing, begin to enter inner space and time.*

*Be aware of the flowing river of eternal time to which your breath belongs.*

*Be aware of your eternal self and of the eternal being of the one you grieve.*

*In the calm quiet, listen: Hear the soft rhythmic pulsing of your heart.*

*Take the time to listen to your heart until you hear it speak its deep desire, its intention for your life in this moment.*

*Let yourself know that our deepest intentions can be very simple, very honest and innocent:*

*May I be grateful for the love I have known.*

*May I see the essence of beauty deep in the face of my beloved as he is dying.*

*May I allow the well of my tears to open.*

*May my grief help me grow more tender.*

*May I have courage to enter the unknown.*

*May my heart not become embittered by my grief.*

*May any bitterness in my heart soften into sadness.*

*May I be in awe of this mystery of living and dying.*

*Let whatever comes to you from deep in your heart be held in the grace of intention.*

*You may whisper your intention each time you meditate.*

*You may listen to and whisper your heart's intention as you open your eyes in the morning and as you close them at night.*

*Be aware of how your intention unfolds and directs your actions during this day.*

*As you meditate on your intentions, trust that they will root deep within you.*

*May your life-giving intentions touch your grief with compassion.*

*May they bring solace to your thoughts and feelings.*

## *In your journal*

YOU MAY WANT TO WRITE A LETTER to your loved one, who has passed or is passing. You may wish to express the words of your heart that hold your intention of how to carry forth the love and life you shared. Something as simple as:

*This morning I gathered wild flowers and placed them into your vase. Your beauty shines through their colors.*

*My heart's desire, my intention, is to honor your spirit and, in doing so, carry you forth.*

# 7.

## *My heart guides me to make final decisions*

WHEN IRREVOCABLE DEATH APPROACHES, we often need to make a decision very quickly, particularly when events occur that could not be foreseen or were for some reason not tended to earlier.

The crystal voice of wisdom in the center of your heart is all you can rely on in such moments. This voice has nothing to do with right or wrong or what should or should not be done. In fact, what you think *should be done* may run totally counter to what you hear when you listen to your inner guidance.

*A brother dies suddenly in a car crash, never having made his burial wishes known.*

*The decision must be made: Shall he be buried or cremated? The family asks the sister closest to the young man to make the decision.*

*Reluctantly, she agrees.*

*How will Susan make this decision? She never discussed burial plans with her brother, so she does not know her brother's wishes. She sleeps on it. The next morning, she sits quietly with her tears, hears her heart speak: "I feel the farm in Vermont is the right place to bury him. It's where he was happiest. Somehow, I know he would want to be cremated and have his ashes buried on the hill under the apple tree."*

*Susan shares this sense of knowing with her family and they breathe a sigh of relief for the rightness of the decision, coming from a sister's heart to honor her brother.*

Sometimes, we must be the one to make the weighty decisions resulting in letting go or holding on to our loved one:

*My father suffered so severe a stroke there was no chance he would survive. The doctors wanted to know if I would consent to put him on kidney dialysis to prolong his life. It was the middle of the night. I was alone with my unconscious father in the emergency room and designated as his health care proxy. There was no one to call, no one to consult. If I did not give my consent for dialysis, my father would be dead by morning.*

*I left the hospital and walked to a church down the street. Looking up to the roof, I saw a beautiful angel lifting a golden trumpet to the heavens. I walked inside and sat down in the quiet candlelight. No tears. No thoughts. No great deliberations. In my heart, I heard the angel's trumpet reaching to the heavens. I sat, waiting for guidance, waiting for that still, small voice of inner knowing. Perhaps this is what some people call prayer, being quiet until one hears. Perhaps the angel's trumpet was lifting my prayer up to the heavens for help.*

*Suddenly, somehow, from somewhere, I received clarity. I heard a voice saying, "Let him go. He never wanted to live this way. He would never choose to suffer. Let him go in peace."*

*Never before had I known the awesome responsibility love must sometimes carry, the decisions that must sometimes be made in the lonely, prayerful silence of love, the intentions that must be honored because they come from the clear seeing of the heart.*

*Returning to the hospital, I told the doctors my decision. One on each side, they put their arms around me, quietly supporting a decision they could not make for me. One of the doctors said, "I know how hard this is. I had to make a decision like this for my own father."*

*Although I had to make this huge decision on my own, I felt supported by this doctor, who reached across professional boundaries to touch me with the embrace of his human experience, heart to heart. Bless the doctors and nurses who recognize and honor the difficult life and death decisions we must sometimes make.*

May you receive the support you need for the difficult end-of-life decisions you may have to make.

## Guided meditation: Listening with my heart for guidance

*DIFFICULT DECISIONS ARE NOT EASY to make, especially if we are too distraught to trust our clarity. In times of crisis, we may wish to ask others to take over the decision-making responsibilities, assuring them we will honor the final decisions they make on our behalf.*

*Or, perhaps we feel we can make the necessary decisions with another's support. It may be just what we need, to sit with another beside us, listening together to the voices of our heart.*

*Whether the decisions you face are large or small, let yourself ask,*

*"What does my loved one need?*

*What is or was my loved one's wish?*

*What does my heart want?*

*What does my heart need?*

*Even if our wishes may differ, what must I do to honor my loved one?"*

*Ask these questions and any others that arise in you.*

*Then be still for as long as you need until the answers come.*

*Sometimes we find ourselves raising our heart up toward some invisible source for guidance, waiting in silence for our depths to receive the help we seek.*

*Let yourself wait to be guided as you sit in stillness.*

*You may need to sit quietly for several minutes, or longer, perhaps for hours or days.*

*You may wish to take a long walk, or meditate, or ask for guidance when you go to sleep.*

*As you close your eyes, you may ask: Please bring me guidance for this difficult decision I must make.*

*When I awake, may I know the direction I need to take on behalf of my loved one.*

*As you wait to receive and to follow the wisdom of your heart, feel the peace of making decisions from the depth of your true being.*

*When we listen to the voice of guidance, we never know exactly where it will come from.*

*It could be the voice of our loved one, who can no longer speak.*

*It could be the voice of God or of an angel, or an ancestor who watches over, or of an invisible-but-felt Wise Self.*

*Sometimes this becoming still, this asking to receive guidance, this waiting for direction to come, is the only way open to us.*

*So, let yourself rest in the trust that you have given your devotion to the decision that you are responsible for making.*

*Bow to honor the wise counsel that comes to answer your call and your heart in its way.*

*As you go on to follow through with your decisions, may you trust that you did your best, guided by your love and by a great love that you trusted in.*

## *In your journal*

SIT QUIETLY WITH A BLANK PAGE of your journal open before you.

In the silence, allow the decision you are being called to make sit somewhere in your body.

Does it sit in your chest, stomach, heart, or head?

Listen to the place in your body speak, then return to your breathing.

Now, allow silence to come and, into the silence, whisper your call for help.

Perhaps, "Please help me know how best to tell the doctors to proceed."

Or, "Please guide me in sitting with my loved one so that we can make this difficult decision together."

Write the question that rises up from your body into the silence and onto the black page.

Then, sit quietly. Hold the question gently. Breathe.

Let go of your thinking mind.

Breathe. Sit in silence until you hear an answer come.

Let the answer come from the flow of your wise heart.

Write both your call for help and what you receive as guidance.

Write any feelings that arise as you sit with this meditation.

Sit in silence and see yourself going forward to follow the guidance you have received.

Allow yourself to feel the dignity and sincerity of carrying out this decision from the depth of your heart.

# 8.

# *I accept grief-rage as part of mourning*

NGER IS A NATURAL FEELING when you are grieving. I call it "grief-rage." You are suffering a profound loss. Your love is powerless. You can do nothing to prevent your loss. You stand in empty time, in empty space, feeling small in this vast universe that gives and takes. In helpless shock, you ask how life can do this to your loved one, to you. How could you be left and your dear one taken away? It all feels like a game of dice, all so random.

Your grief-rage is an expression of the depth of your loss and anguished helplessness and love. Grief, rage wrapped in anger, is a cry, a scream of protest, against the blinding reality that *death* has taken the living from you.

Grief-rage at the loss of someone we love needs to be felt, needs to be expressed. It is a very powerful force that is moving through you. Your grief-rage waits to move, needs to move, for if we don't allow ourselves to feel and express it, a great surge of energy becomes lodged inside, oftentimes speaking through the body in symptoms of illness and other ways, demanding that our attention be given.

*When my daughter died, I became very quiet. I went dead in my shocked grief. I could not cry. My grief-rage froze me.*

*One day, in early fall, I walk on the beach, alone. The beach is empty. The waves are loud, their crashing sounds envelope me. Somehow, I feel safe, held in what seems larger than my grief-rage. I begin to cry. I continue walking slowly along the beach, weeping. I walk and weep for a long time. Slowly, my tears give way to screams. They have a life of their own. I scream louder and louder. What begins as anger turns to anguish, pure animal grief.*

*My screams pierce my frozen self, try to tear through the invisible curtain separating me from my daughter. The waters and heavens are vast enough to receive my bottomless grief-rage. I lie down on the sand and weep and weep. The waves roll in and out. Their rhythm soothes me and my grief rage softens into the rhythmic bleating cries of an innocent animal.*

*Slowly, I come back to life. My screams deliver me back and thaw the prison frozen grief-rage has built around my body and soul. I lie there on the beach, my body of grief-anger, my anguish comforted and softened into a vulnerable grief moving through me, in and out, in and out, with the waves. Then the waves roll out with the tides, carrying the ocean of tears I have cried. The waters are quiet now, a mirror of shimmering light as I lay on the shoreline spent, held by a vast blue heaven of mercy.*

If we allow it, grief-rage comes naturally. You may feel angry with your loved one or angry with yourself. You may feel angry at life, at God, at death. If your anger can soften, its imprisoning walls will soften as well. Grief-rage not softened deadens into grief gone hard, imprisoning us in a frozen state.

Once given space to move, your grief-rage can slowly turn into a soft grief. This turning from hard to soft takes its time to slowly release the tight grip of holding. As you allow your hard feelings to soften, your body will not need to carry the protective armor of tightened muscles, a shut-down nervous system, a freezing of the rhythmic flow of your natural, animal body.

As you allow your grief-rage to be heard without judgment, without demand that it be different, allow it to scream up to the heavens. You have the best chance of reaching the soft belly feelings of your hidden grief and releasing them to be held in the spirit of great love.

Held in the Great Love, may your broken heart, in time, slowly open again to hold others in our world, who are also crying out the anger and rage of their grief.

## Guided meditation: Being with my grief-rage

SIT QUIETLY AND PREPARE YOURSELF to find and meet your grief-rage.

You need a safe place for this meditation, a place where you can allow strong emotions to arise if they are ready to.

Ask yourself if you need someone to be beside you in this release and healing. Perhaps a friend, minister, spiritual guide, or bereavement counselor? Would you feel more comfortable writing in your journal?

You can ask your grief-rage, "What do you need?" Sense how grateful your grief-rage is to receive your non-judging presence as you allow it to move through you, letting its freezing soften or, hearing that it will not soften yet and must stay hard in anger for now.

Know that your rage is part of your grief.

Let yourself listen to it, to the feelings, thoughts, sensations of your body.

*Your anger may have words.*

*If it has no words, it may have sounds: a howling, a scream, a sob, a wail, a moan.*

*You may allow your body to move the energies that are in your grief-anger, allowing them to find expression and release through your body movements.*

*Do you need to release your feelings physically? If so, you can use pillows, pound on them with your fists as rage comes.*

*Or, you can sit quietly and listen in stillness for the sound of your grief rage and watch, as in a waking dream, for its movements. See where you are, perhaps in a place vast enough to receive your cries, or small enough to hold and protect you.*

*You may find yourself moving with your sound, body swaying, head moving "No, No," falling over like a rag doll, raising up arms, lifting them to search the heavens for help.*

*Or crouching to reach the terror wrapped in your anger, the terror of being left to go on without your loved one. Stay crouched until its movement naturally unfolds the energies wanting to be released and known.*

*Stay with the natural movements of your innocent, spontaneous body.*

*Be with the consoling rhythms that move through animals and little children and any of us who allow our grief sounds to begin to have their natural flow.*

*And if your grief-rage doesn't want to move, is not ready, know it may be serving you, protecting you from feeling the "too-muchness" of the full force of the raging pain of your grief.*

*Don't judge yourself if your grief-anger lingers.*

*Let it have its softest and loudest sounds, its words that may whisper or scream themselves up into the heavens that are large enough to hold them.*

*Perhaps you can find an outer place to go to or a place within the space of imagination that waits for you to come.*

*We are alone in our grief-rage. And we are not alone when we acknowledge that our grief-rage is shared with so many others in our world whose hearts are also crying with a rage for their loss. You may find yourself whispering to someone or to somewhere in the world: I am not alone. You out there.*

*You are not alone. We are humans together on this journey of loss and love. I know you. You know me.*

## *In your journal*

AFTER YOU HAVE LISTENED TO WHERE in your body your grief rage lives just now, moving or held, let it speak onto your open journal page.

In your journal, you can find the words or draw the images of your grief rage.

Choose the colors that reflect it. Allow your hand, your arm, your body, and your breathing to move through the colors onto the page.

Title a blank page: I am your grief rage.

Let it speak. Let it write itself.

If your grief rage is too raw for words, perhaps you can place the color of your rage upon your fingers and let your fingers move your rage from your body onto the page. Perhaps your fingers want to jab onto the page, perhaps your fist wants to pound the colors you have placed there.

These are ways to give your grief rage the space to breathe and move, to begin to tell its story.

Become aware of any comfort that may come as you write and

draw your grief rage onto the page.

Feel and sense the comfort of release moving, breathing in your body.

Listen to the voice of the comfort. Let it speak to you and write on to the page.

Draw the movement of the comfort that is opening as you make space for your grief rage.

See and listen to anything shifting in the energies of your grief rage as it is touched by comfort.

Write as you track the movement of your grief rage. You may find yourself coming to the story your grief rage wants to tell. Listen to the story and write it.

# 9.

# *I forgive, and I accept forgiveness*

IN THE ACT OF FORGIVENESS, LIFE IS CLEANSED. Until we have forgiven, we cannot let be, let go, or go on. We remain caught in the past. Our attachment to our hurt and anger becomes a prison.

*Charles has not spoken to or seen his mother for 20 years, ever since she rejected him when he told her he was gay. But he thinks of her and speaks of her with hatred every day. Even his dreams of her are filled with feelings of hate. After she dies, he finally relents. At the behest of his family, he attends her funeral, taking this final opportunity to feel the grief that sits under his anger, grief for her rejection of him.*

*Charles begins to make peace and, in doing so, he gains the freedom to go on with his life with a deep sadness of having missed the mother love he longed for. In living with his grief, Charles leaves the bitter prison of his hatred and accepts the past as it was.*

Just as with every other aspect of grief, the process of forgiveness cannot be rushed. It has its own rhythm. It takes time to work through feelings of anger because they cover a well of hurt, of tears, of unfulfilled needs and hopes. In order for us to come to forgiveness, we need to uncover buried grief of unfulfilled longings, feel the depth of hurt, and discover we can bear it and live through it. Like a wound scabbed over, our hurt wants to open and be given air. The pain of a tightly closed wound opening leads to healing, to new hope and new beginnings.

Pride is often the greatest obstacle to forgiveness. We fear losing face, losing our dignity. Perhaps we feel the person we refuse to forgive has violated our basic values, our sense of what is right and good, of how people should be with one another. As we unwrap the shield of our pride that covers our deep hurt, we are able to touch how, deep within us, at the center of our hurt and anger and pride, there is a sacred longing. Once we touch that longing, we are touching our dignity and our life-giving movement, which is always stronger than the force of pride and anger.

*In time, Charles comes to touch his deep and sacred longing for his mother's love and respect for his sexual orientation at the bottom of his anger. He goes on living in the dignity of his essential being and out of this comes forgiveness of the limits of his mother's love.*

Forgiveness does not condone or condemn someone's behavior. Forgiveness is a process by which we long to be free of the hurt and hatred that have broken our spirit. We long for a sense of wholeness.

When we let our pride fall away, we realize we, too, have wounded others, been loving and hateful, kind and selfish, caring and insensitive. This awareness brings us a deep and indestructible ground of dignity upon which to stand, a dignity that comes from owning all parts of ourselves, the full common humanity we share with others.

From the humility of knowing how imperfect we are and how imperfect our love is, we gain the capacity for compassion for others and ourselves. Out of compassion comes forgiveness for being frail human beings. Forgiveness says, "We are each clay vessels, soon to break. We can only carry the intention not to hurt another, knowing how precious life is and how vulnerable we each are. Because we are imperfect humans, we will hurt and be hurt and, again, we will ask and give forgiveness. This is the way the heart opens."

In the process of forgiving, as you allow your hard anger to turn to the soft hurting, you may wish to share your feelings, no longer to blame, but rather to bare your heart to the other and to cleanse and renew your connection.

You may wonder whether someone who is dying can withstand this healing process. Perhaps not, but I know what I want most in my life is for people to be real with me, not to live a lie with me. When I am dying, I cannot imagine wanting anything other than the naked love of healing repair, given tenderly and with a love that holds my hand and holds relationship and its wounding and its healing as sacred.

"Real" does not mean merely smiling, being kind or peaceful. Real may also mean pain, anger, and tears. To be real is to be openly and mindfully who one is, challenging intent to hurt or seek revenge, bringing awareness to wash what blocks our open-hearted presence. Perhaps your loved one is too ill to engage in this process with you. You may simply be able to provide a gentle, "I'm sorry for. . ." or "I forgive you for. . ." or a touch or a look that says, "All is cleansed of that wound, all is reconciled between us. We are good. We are at peace together."

Truth telling can be very tender, tender to oneself and to the other. It is the tenderness of truth held and offered in one's open hand that holds forgiveness and allows going on with dignity. The truth telling that brings forgiveness can also be spoken with your soft eyes looking into the eyes of your loved one or with the language of a soft touch with the intention of washing away what has wounded with forgiveness. In Japan, there is a practice of mending cracked vessels with gold. Forgiveness is that gold, which fills the cracks between us.

Perhaps the two of you cannot outwardly reconcile a hurt. The process may take longer than your loved one has the time for. Know that it is possible for you to go through the process of forgiveness alone for the two of you. Just the wish, the intention, that is in you to do so will soften the movement of your heart, and your loved one will sense this movement.

Sometimes it takes a long time to forgive, perhaps a lifetime. We each go through this journey in our own way and at our own pace. You can begin by planting a seed-intention that says, "I want to forgive.

I do not know how. My heart, please help me. Please help me move from the protective shell of my hardened heart into my broken openheartedness."

## Guided meditation: Planting a seed of forgiveness

SEE YOURSELF STANDING IN FRONT of a mirror that is oval and has two sides to it.

See that the mirror has a golden frame and stands in the middle of the room.

See yourself standing in front of the side of the mirror of being unforgiving.

See yourself holding fast to "never forgiving" the wrong that has been committed against you.

See and feel your face, your body, your breathing.

*See yourself going on into the future in this way.*

*Know how it is to go on in the way of never forgiving.*

*Now, go to stand on the other side of the mirror.*

*See yourself standing before the side of the mirror in which you see yourself forgiving.*

*See yourself wanting to go on feeling free within yourself.*

*See yourself letting go of holding tight to past hurt and anger.*

*See yourself in this mirror.*

*See and sense your face, your body, your breathing*

*See yourself going on into the future in this way of forgiveness.*

*Be aware of yourself on each side of the mirror, carrying the full truth of your struggle with coming to forgiveness.*

*Let yourself know this as the human struggle in each of us.*

*You can carry this meditation with you when you are in the presence of the one who is ill and facing death when you are aware of your difficulty to touch forgiveness in yourself even as you long for it.*

*At such a time, take a moment, take a deep breath, and see yourself moving from the mirror of being unforgiving to the side of forgiving. Go back and forth. Sense your body, your breathing on each side of the mirror.*

*Move from one side of the mirror to the other with an awareness of unfolding the seed intention of your soul to live toward a future in which forgiveness is possible.*

*In this moment, feel how it is to have even one drop of the healing and wholeness of forgiveness live in your body.*

*Be aware of your face, your mouth, your eyes as you take even a moment to be in the heart of forgiveness.*

## *In your journal*

ON TWO FACING PAGES, DRAW the oval mirrors with the gold frames.

On one page, draw the mirror of not forgiving. Write in this mirror everything you tell yourself about never forgiving.

Listen. Accept all that you hear in this voice.

Feel your body and your breathing.

On the facing page, draw the mirror of forgiveness with its gold frame.

In this mirror, write everything that wants to be spoken from your forgiving self.

Sense and feel your body and breathing as you write into this mirror.

During the week, go back and forth between the two mirrors.

Be aware if anything changes as you practice this meditation.

# 10.

## *A story waits to be told*

WHILE I SAT AT MY FATHER'S SIDE as he lay dying, I recalled how he used to sit at my side when I was a child because I was afraid of the dark. To honor him, after he died, I wrote this story:

*Once there was a little girl who was afraid of the dark. One night, in her bedroom, she found herself in a terrible, frightening darkness. She cowered as a tight fist of fear knotted in her stomach. She felt completely alone as the darkness grew larger than the world and threatened to engulf her.*

*The little girl closed her eyes in terror. Maybe if she made herself very small and shut her eyes tight, she could hide from the dark. But that didn't work. Even after becoming smaller and smaller, with her eyes sealed shut, she still shivered with fear.*

*She had a thought: Maybe her father was in the room with her, maybe he had come to her rescue. She opened her eyes, hoping she would see him, but he wasn't there. She was still alone in the dark. She called to her father, "Daddy, Daddy, please come to me. I'm so afraid of the dark!" Her father heard her call and came to her.*

*The little girl's father sat next to her on her bed for a long time. He put kisses on her head and held her little hand in his big hands. He told her he would not leave until she felt safe. Then he got up and placed a shining, glittering silver star on the ceiling of her room and said, "Of all the stars that shine, this one is your star. Whenever it is dark for you, whenever you begin to feel afraid, just look up at your star, twinkling bright." He asked the little girl, "Do you feel safe enough in the dark for me to stand just outside your door while you get to know the dark a little bit more?"*

*"Yes," she said, and while he stood just outside the door, the little girl began to explore the darkness in her room. At first, she was frightened and sucked her tongue between her lips, just to feel something was there. And then she remembered her father, just outside her door and she remembered her star on the ceiling.*

*Bravely, she walked, holding her teddy bear, to a dark corner of the room. The dark was thick as velvet. She reached her teddy's paw out into the darkness and the darkness covered her like a warm, velvet shawl. She gathered the shawl around her and around her teddy and she looked up at her twinkling star. She thought of her father, standing outside her door, helping her get to know the darkness. The little girl sat down on the floor. She sat in the quiet darkness, wrapped in it, quiet and safe for a long time, then called out to her father, "You can go now, Daddy."*

*When the little girl grew up, she loved to sit quietly in the darkness. It was like music to her. Eventually, her father grew very old. One night, as she was tending him, he called out to her, "Daughter, now it is I who am afraid of the dark. I am afraid to close my eyes for I do not know where the darkness will take me."*

*She went to him and held his right hand in her big hands. She kissed his brow. She stroked his bald head and, slowly, he closed his eyes and rested into the velvet darkness, a darkness that seemed like the darkness of the whole universe, where he was all alone. The daughter held his hand and told him to look at the light on the other side of the darkness, to look at the star, his star, a guiding light to lead him to those he loved who were already safely in the great light, who were already holding his left hand on the other side of the veil. She whispered the names of his mother and his father, his brothers, his grandfather and grandmother, and especially the name of his beloved granddaughter.*

*Then, as she kissed his brow, she heard her father say to her very softly, "I am not afraid of the dark now. You can go now, Daughter. I see a light greater than the light of the little star I gave you so long ago. It is the light of a great lighthouse, guiding its ship to come home. Thank you for holding my hand until I could see the great light. It is like the light of the lighthouse I used to love on the beach where we went when you were a little girl. Only, this lighthouse shines ever brighter and never stops shining."*

*And then he slipped into the velvet waters of darkness carrying him to the other shore. And the daughter knows that whenever she finds solace in the music of her darkness, she will sense her father, peaceful in the music of his light.*

There are stories sitting patiently inside each one of us, waiting to be told.

Our stories become a vessel into which we can place our loss, our love, our darkness and light.

On the Path of Grief, our stories hold us together, help us understand, and give meaning to what is happening to our loved one and to ourselves.

Some say writing our story can save our life. Certainly, our stories that tell of our grief journey can bring back and hold our soul that may feel lost to us, waiting to be found.

## Guided meditation: Singing my story

SIT QUIETLY.

*Let yourself become open to the story that sits within you. Listen for the words.*

*Speak them when they come. . . "Once". . .listen to what comes next. . . "Once upon a time. . . ."*

*It helps to speak our stories and write them as tales.*

*Telling the tale takes us into what I call "dream language."*

*Dream language expresses our feelings, the story that sits deep inside, not just the sequence of events.*

*Dream language finds the story sitting in our heart, waiting to be told.*

*You may find yourself beginning to write your story, thinking you are finished.*

*And then, during the day, or as you are falling asleep at night, more will come.*

*If this happens, continue to write your story in your journal.*

*Don't wait too long to do so, for, like a dream, the story that rises up from your deep self can easily fade.*

## In your journal

Sit in your space of solace, your journal open before you.

Close your eyes, breathe, and listen. What are the first words of your story?

Let them rise up from out of your inner quiet.

Speak them aloud. As you speak the words, let them speak for you and write them down in your journal.

Trust and see where they lead you.

If it feels right for you, continue to write for at least 15 minutes without taking your pen off the page.

Just keep writing, especially when you most want to stop.

Return to your journal each day and continue writing for 10 or 15 minutes without lifting your pen from the page. Let your story flow.

You may be surprised to see what comes.

Even if what comes onto the page is painful, you may feel some sense of healing, some sense of peace and wholeness brought to you by telling your story.

This is the healing gift of storytelling.

# II.

# *Finding solace in the natural world*

SIMON'S BROTHER, CARL, FINALLY LOST *his long battle with AIDS. On the night he died, Simon took Carl to the emergency room. When the busy staff told him to wait outside while they tended to Carl, Simon screamed at them, "I can't leave him! You can't separate me from my brother!" Simon sat crying in the waiting room until the doctor came to tell Simon that Carl would not survive the night.*

*Simon sat through the night, holding his brother's hand, quietly singing his favorite songs to him. Carl died as the sun rose. Simon left the hospital. Not knowing how he left his brother, Carl walked—lost— through the familiar streets, disembodied, like a ghost. He wanted to turn around, go back to the hospital, go back to his brother, but he kept walking, dazed and bewildered.*

*Simon moved through the streets like a sleepwalker and eventually found himself in a park, where he wandered aimlessly, feeling removed from himself and everything around him. The world moved dreamlike: Parents hurried their children to school;*

*dogs tugged at leashes; joggers and cyclists sped by. No one looked at him, did not know he had just left his brother dead in a hospital emergency room. The world moved before him as if in a dream, in which he was invisible, without substance, in a land called Loss.*

*Simon's thoughts turned to a time when, as a child, he had become separated from his mother and brother in a large department store. He remembered feeling stricken with terror, feeling small in a vast and suddenly strange world, with no big brother's hand to hold. He felt the same way in that moment, stumbling through the park, no brother's hand to hold. His tears had no end. Carl's hand would never be there for him again.*

*Simon came to a lake. It was very quiet. He sat at the lake's edge staring up at the heavens, staring out over the water. His tears quieted as he watched the lake turn around a bend and disappear out of sight. It seemed to go on and on, beyond where he could see. The heavens went on and on and then disappeared beyond the horizon.*

*Through a veil of dazed grief, Simon's eyes rested on the water, on the endless rippling. It seemed to him there was one wave, flowing on and on. Something about the movement of the water, the ceaseless flow of the one wave going on and on, ever present, ever disappearing, flowed into Simon and soothed his breathing and held his tears.*

*That summer, Simon returned to the same spot at the lake every day. It became his place of solace. He sat gazing out over the water and at the vast sky every morning and every evening. One day, as Simon sat quietly by the lake, he sensed the water speaking to him: "The flow never stops. There is only one wave, flowing on and on.*

*You can't see the water rippling beyond the bend of the lake. You can't see the sky continuing beyond the horizon. You can't see your brother beyond where you left him, beyond this life. But the water, the sky, your brother, all go on and on in ways you only now begin to understand."*

*As these words flowed into him, the light and the breeze filtering through the trees touched him with the beauty and primal rhythms of nature. Simon still ached with grief, but, by summer's end, he felt less lost and alone. Something had shifted, and he could feel his brother close by. In these moments, in the rhythmic movement of the endless wave, he felt his brother's presence, the touch of his hand. He could feel and sense the endless flowing rhythm of all life. Like a web that holds all creation in seamless inter-being, Simon's taking refuge at the lake brought the rhythm and flow of all life into the cracks of his broken-hearted grief and numbed body.*

*Simon began to understand, in his moments by the lake, how death is not an ending and birth is not a beginning. And while he didn't fully understand, as none of us can, he was comforted by a glimmer of vague knowing, a sense of life going on and on, a feeling of his brother being on the other side of a thin veil, only a whisper away.*

## *Guided meditation: Finding solace in the rhythms of nature*

SIT QUIETLY LET YOUR EYES SOFTLY CLOSE.

*Be aware of your breath, breathing in, breathing out.*

*See yourself walking in a calm, quiet place in nature, perhaps near the water or into a garden, or into a deep forest or silent desert.*

*See where you have come to. See all that surrounds you.*

*Be still and notice a place in which you can sit.*

*Sit in the spot you have found and listen to the sounds of nature all around you: a bird singing, a breeze moving through swaying branches, water flowing.*

*Breathe in this place of beauty and solace.*

*Breathe with all that is living and breathing in this place in nature.*

*Feel yourself a part of all of creation.*

*Breathe with the grasses and trees and with every living thing.*

*As you breathe, let your heart open.*

*Allow everything arising within to just be: sadness, sweet memories, despair, hope, loss, gratitude.*

*Accept all that comes to be felt, all a part of creation.*

*Feel your soft, animal body allowing every feeling to move through you.*

*Listen to the breeze move in the trees.*

*Listen. Hear what the breeze is saying to you.*

*Whisper back what you hear.*

*Breathe the healing beauty and rhythm of nature into your body and spirit.*

*Breathe into the places of your body needing to be touched by nature's solace.*

*Now, in the stillness, hear the rhythmic sound of your breathing.*

*Know how your breathing is part of all living, breathing nature.*

*Feel and sense how nature's rhythms restore the rhythms of your body and soul.*

*Know how you are a part of the ceaseless rhythm of all living things.*

*Sense how healing it is to sit in your spot in nature.*

*If you cannot find a place in nature near home, a park or beach, some green space, know that you can always come to this place that is yours to sit in during your time in your quiet place at home.*

## *In your journal*

IF YOU CAN COME TO A PLACE IN NATURE that is consoling to you, be there with your journal beside you.

You may wish to stroll until you stop at a spot that calls to you to come and sit.

If you are not near a place in nature, you can sit in your space of solitude, perhaps with a lovely plant or a vase of flowers nearby, or simply the sunlight streaming in through a window.

Or, you can sit in the place of nature you came to in your meditation.

Sit quietly and be aware of the beauty and the brevity of the things of nature surrounding you.

Sense your breathing coming into a rhythm with the ephemeral beauty of the natural world.

Be still, breathe, and allow your feelings to open to move through you.

Whatever they are, allow them.

Be aware of any feelings in your body moving through you with their natural rhythm, perhaps a rhythm of sorrow to solace and back again.

Allow the rhythm of your nature in this moment to move through you just as the breeze moves through the trees.

Take your time to write whatever wants to come to the blank page.

May you feel a sense of gratitude for the flowing rhythms of all nature, including your own.

May the rhythms of nature touch you with some solace for your sorrow.

# 12.

## *I help the child within*

I HAVE A LITTLE FRIEND I LOVE VERY MUCH. *Her name is Maria. When she was three years old, she loved to hold the leash of my dog Blue on our walks through the meadow. I often sat under the maple tree and watched them run and play together. At night, on the telephone, Maria and I had our Blue ritual, "Where is Blue-Blue?" she asked.*

*"Blue-Blue is sleeping now, but he sends you a kiss." And I'd send the kiss through the phone to Maria.*

*That spring, Blue became very ill. One day, he let me know with his soft eyes that he was ready to go. I wrapped him in his blanket and took him to the vet. I held him while he slowly relaxed and left his little body. Silence surrounded us. I kissed him goodbye.*

*That night on the phone, Maria said, "I know Blue-Blue went to heaven but, where is he? Is he sleeping? Where's my kiss?" Maria spent many months trying to figure out death and where Blue had gone, but it was all beyond her. We buried his ashes under the tree in the meadow and planted flowers over them. Still Maria asked, "Where is Blue-Blue?" Eventually, she stopped asking and Blue seemed to disappear for her.*

*One cold March day, Maria and I went for a walk in the meadow and stopped at "our" maple tree. One small, red bud grew out of the ground over Blue's grave site.*

*Maria ran to it, kissed it, and said, "Oh, look! Blue sent me a beautiful, red flower."*

There is this child in each of us trying to fathom someone being here, being gone, coming back, not coming back. We still play versions of those hide-and-seek, peek-a-boo games children love to play to master the comings and goings, reassuring themselves that when something goes away it comes back.

But then there are those times in childhood when what has gone cannot be brought back by just dropping our hands from our eyes. Grandparents die, parents separate, our dear friends move away, pets grow old and "disappear." These separations make profound impressions on the child's soul, impressions that affect our adult reactions to loss.

*I remember making butter in kindergarten. I remember how carefully, proudly I carried it home in a small bowl. It shone in my hands like the sun, warm and golden. I had made sunshine! Soon after this glorious day, my parents separated. The sun slipped away. Everything went dark, and I believed there was nothing I could do to ever bring back the sun.*

As adults, the deaths of those we love carry echoes of our early experiences of loss and abandonment.

When my father left, I dreamed I would return from school to find him sitting at the kitchen table waiting for me with milk and cookies, just as he had before he left. After my daughter died, I dreamed over and over how I would come home to find her running to meet me as I opened the door. She would be there waiting for me and we would have our milk and graham crackers together. Upon waking, I felt a cut of loss in my solar plexus, as fresh as the first cut of losing my father echoing in the loss of my daughter.

With each major loss, we fall through the cracks of time back into the unhealed wounds of grief from our childhoods. The deeper the childhood hurt, the deeper we fall into the depths of that wound until we find ourselves in a dark crater without exit. At the bottom of this crater, the child we were still waits for someone to find her, lift her out, and help her go on.

That child waits forever for our help to unravel and separate the traumatic losses of the past from the painful loss of the present. If your present loss is traumatic—on top of the past traumatic loss you suffered as a child—it may be wise to seek the help of a grief therapist to guide you through this complicated past grief opening into your present grief.

## Guided meditation: Sitting with my inner child self

CLOSE YOUR EYES FOR A FEW MOMENTS. *Open them. Allow them to stay half open, half closed. Come to your breathing. Breathe in, breathe out.*

*Let yourself drift on your long exhalation until your breath becomes a path.*

*Follow the path until you come to stand in front of a closed door.*

*Open the door and see a child standing there, waiting for you.*

*Know this is the child within you, your child self, waiting for you to bring comfort for a loss suffered long ago.*

*Come close to the child, look into his eyes, sense what she is feeling.*

*Does she reach out to welcome your presence? Is she too frozen to move?*

*How old is the child? What does he look like? What is she wearing?*

*Look into her eyes, what do you see there?*

*Hear what he says to you in words or with her eyes or body.*

*Perhaps she says, "Please don't leave me alone again. Who will hold me?*

*I'm afraid of the world staying dark forever.*

*Did you leave me because I did something bad?*

*Will I always be alone? Will you stay with me now?"*

*What is the child within saying to you? Listen. Sit with this child who is still you.*

*Perhaps she will allow you to hold her or will come sit in your lap.*

*Be there for this child who has waited so long for you to come.*

*Perhaps it will take time for the two of you to come close.*

*Let her cry. Let him be angry.*

*Accept whatever this child needs to feel, to share.*

*Sense where this child lives inside your body and has lived for so long.*

*Place your hand there, sense your hand letting the child know you are present and will not leave her alone ever again.*

*Give your child self the loving presence she longs for, the love you would give any child who is hurting.*

*Let your grownup self speak to your child self with all the wisdom of your years, with all you are now.*

*Sense its sacred longing and say to the child: "You will never be alone again, I will always be here for you."*

*Let yourself know that what you give to the child now is all that was ever needed long ago.*

*Let your child self relax into the compassionate embrace. Feel your body relax.*

*Know how you are freeing your grown self to live in the present and to feel your present sorrow unwound from the incomplete mourning of the past.*

*Feel the blessing of completing healing for the grief of your young self.*

## *In your journal*

GIVE YOURSELF THE TIME IN YOUR SPACE of solitude to write the story of being with the child within you, who has waited so long for you to find her.

You may write the story as if it were a dream you have recalled or as a tale waiting and wanting to be told.

Write in 15-minute intervals without lifting your hand from the page.

In this way, you help your story to flow out of you and do not go up into your thinking, editing mind.

As you write this story of your early loss and grief, know that you are bringing healing to your early experience that has lived in your body for so long. As you write, be aware of how you are unwinding old grief from your body and your nervous system and restoring your well-being.

Telling your childhood story now is also freeing your heart to hold your present grief, to hold your loved one in the honoring of a present freed of the past.

# 13.

## *I observe my rituals*

I VISITED MY DEAR FRIEND SHIRLEY *when she was gravely ill. We sat at the table with her two granddaughters watching what was happening in the terrarium: A molting snake, moving very slowly, was easing out of her skin, one small piece at a time. With about two inches of old skin left to shed, the snake suddenly stopped moving. She seemed not quite ready to release her old familiar skin entirely. She remained motionless. We left to go out to dinner.*

*When we returned, we saw only the discarded skin on the floor of the terrarium. The snake had retreated to the castle in the center of the terrarium. "Let's throw the skin away," said six-year-old Julie.*

*"No, Julie," Shirley told her, "let's leave the skin be for a while. The snake is very vulnerable as she gets used to not having a skin. Let's leave her and her skin alone as they slowly separate from one another."*

*As we watched the snake shed its familiar skin, I believe Shirley knew she was shedding hers as well. She understood so well the time needed by the snake to let go of its old life. I understand now that Shirley, like the snake, was living in an unknown space of transition between living and dying. Somehow, it is in our nature to mark our transitions from one form of identity to another by enacting ritual. Shirley created a ritual for the snake to honor a slow parting from its skin.*

*Shirley died two months later. From the time she shed her skin to the time of her burial, family and friends sat with her spirit as she separated from her body. While I sat beside Shirley, I was overcome with the sense of someone being birthed. In the long hours of her transition, I sensed something very active and sacred taking place, a palpable sense of Shirley's transition from this life into an ineffable place I could only dimly sense. Her breathing slowed, became less frequently, until it ceased, and all was silent. Life had left. We continued to sit in our circle for some time, held in the sacred silence of this luminous mystery of life's passing.*

*We guarded her spirit, in her own castle of light, so she could get used to the shedding of her life. This was a ritual that held all of us, in body and in spirit. One of us hummed, another sat in quiet prayer, another in his own rhythm of weeping. We sat that way for about six hours, as we were told that is how long it takes the spirit to depart from the container of the body.*

Rituals provide a container into which the full flood of our grief and our love can flow. Our rituals place a protective circle of solace around both the living and the dying. The circle of ritual comforts and holds us while the mortal aspects of the one we love are releasing. We may sense the eternal sparks of their soul separating from their physical body. Our religious rituals tell us what to do and how to do it at a time when we are floundering in loss. There are those we follow that arise out of the ritual wisdom of the heart.

*Now, Shirley is in a plain pine box. The coffin is lowered into the earth. Each of us begins to shovel earth over the coffin. Each shovelful hits the coffin with an unrelenting heavy and rhythmic sound that stuns our hearts: the stark sound of the reality of death and burial, the ritual sound of dust to dust.*

*Slowly, the coffin is covered with earth. Some cry loudly, some softly. Shirley's daughter, Paula, quietly chants, "Mommy, mommy, mommy," over and over again as she holds her children and they hold her. Paula's rhythmic chant is a ritual holding.*

*We stand in a circle. Together, we face the sorrow and the solace of our shared moments. We hold one another, and this holding is itself ritual holding us. Although we are each alone with our personal loss, we are not alone and that means everything.*

*I notice a yellow flower bud on the ground near the still-open grave. Someone is about to crush it underfoot. I bend, lift it, and give it to Julie, who is reaching for it at the same time. She releases it into the grave. It floats, sparkling sunlight, down onto the covering of dark earth, a last touch of blessing. This, too, is a moment of ritual, this flower reaching to the still-open space, about to be sealed forever.*

If it is possible for you and your loved one to sit together before death comes, you may share the profound experience of creating an end-of-life ritual together. If you are informed of your loved one's end-of-life wishes, you will have the privilege of carrying them out. If not, you may wish to create a ritual by listening to your heart and the hearts of those close to you.

Make the space and time for each of you to share what ritual will most reflect your love and the essence of your loved one. Perhaps the burial or cremation rituals of your religion will guide the way. If not, trust, as you sit together with your inner circle of family, closest friends, and perhaps a member of the clergy, that together you will co-create a ritual revealing what is true for each of you and for your loved one.

Know you are participating in a most sacred ancient ritual of releasing the body and spirit of your loved one, going with your loved one as far as you can go. In your ritual, you are standing in the space of shedding your physical connections while weaving cords of spiritual connection that will go on forever.

## *Guided meditation: A ritual for my loved one*

COME TO YOUR QUIET SPACE *and take the time to sit in silence.*

*You may sit alone or with others who are closest to you and to the one who is dying or has just died.*

*As you sit quietly, hold the intention to receive guidance for the ritual that will most express your love and honoring of the life of the one who is gone.*

*As you sit, be with your breathing. Be open to whatever comes.*

*At first, there may be tears and the ache of grief. Or just silence.*

*Let it all be, returning over and over to your breathing.*

*And then, close your eyes and just drift with your breathing, until you enter the space of dreaming while awake.*

*In your waking dream, find yourself in a space where a ritual is happening for your loved one.*

*Your waking dream may take you to the ocean or to a forest, perhaps to a familiar place you shared with your loved one in nature.*

*As you stand in this spot you have come to, take your time and watch the ritual that you yourself are performing. Watch as you would watch in a dream.*

*You may see yourself planting a tree of remembrance, one you can come to sit under on the anniversaries of your loved one's passing.*

*Or, in your waking dream, you may see yourself travelling somewhere far away, carrying your loved one's ashes to a place he had always wanted to travel to.*

*Even if you cannot physically travel to this place, let yourself know and feel that going there in your waking dream is an expression of your heart's intention to honor your loved one's deep desire.*

*Or, as you sit quietly, you may ask your loved one, "Tell me, what do you wish as a ritual that will express my love, our love, and help you be at peace as you release? Please, tell us so that we may hold the thread of loving as you are unwinding yourself from this physical life."*

*You may hear yourself whispering something like: "Thank you my dear one for sharing life with me.*

*May you know peace, and may you know that your memory will always be a blessing. By this ritual, you are honored and loved for the essence of your being and for all that you have given while alive."*

## *In your journal*

YOU MAY WISH TO HAVE YOUR JOURNAL open beside you as you enter your waking dream so that you can record what ritual for your loved one you came to.

Write your waking dream as clearly as you can so that it becomes a guide for carrying out the ritual you came to in a way that recalls all the small details of honoring your loved one.

If you have been unable to find your ritual in the waking dream meditation, you may wish to write at the top of your journal page: Please bring me a ritual of honoring the life of the one dear to me who has left this life.

Then sit with your eyes closed, come to your breathing, and wait.

When it feels right, take your pencil to the page and begin to write in a flowing way, keeping your hand on the page, for 10 to 15 minutes. Keep writing even if you wish to stop.

See what comes. Perhaps you will be surprised to see what ritual comes to you. And if none comes, allow that to be. Perhaps it is not time to receive a ritual. Perhaps you may wish to ask for help from someone you are close to in creating one. Let yourself honor what your wishes are, without pressure or obligation.

# 14.

# *I help the child within to grieve*

AURA WAS SEVEN WHEN HER FATHER *became ill and was hospitalized. He reassured her he would come home soon and asked her to write a little story she could read to him when he returned. A few days later, Laura's mother returned from the hospital, her head bent, her face tear-stained, held up by two of Laura's uncles. Laura did not ask, and no one told her, but she understood: Her father would not be coming home to hear the story she had written for him.*

*When Laura, now an adult, looks back, she sees how that scene, that time of losing her father, that grief, that frightened little girl, are frozen within her. She never cried, she never asked what happened to her father. She never witnessed any part of his dying. She never attended his funeral. No one spoke to her about his death or helped her speak her feelings. Silence filled the empty spaces and froze her grief. Laura's grief left unaddressed went underground and remained waiting beneath the ice.*

There is nothing as chilling and isolating at a time of loss as sensing something terrible, but not really knowing what is going on. The child who cannot partake in the process of grief, according to his capacity, has no choice other than to put painful feelings into cold storage. These frozen feelings only begin to thaw with the help of someone who can be present to that still confused, hurting child to help her through the process she couldn't go through in actual childhood.

No matter how old we are, a death will reawaken the child within who may still carry the wounds of first losses. When death comes to the family, our child within needs to be seen, heard, and comforted just as the children surrounding us. When someone dies, children need us to share the truth of what is happening to the degree they are intellectually and emotionally ready to take in the reality. Children need support to ask questions, to feel connected to the process of grief, to share tears and create memories. Children need to be held in the safe circle of family, to feel surrounded by contact and warmth, even if the warmth is sad.

If we did not have this comfort of safety surrounding our childhood losses, we can create that now in the time of our present loss. We can do this because the child within waits forever for the completion of its mourning to come.

*Laura and I created a ritual in which her hidden inner child was able to relive the loss of her father in a healing way. We entered this ritual in the space of imagination where time flows freely from the present to the past and back again, in which living the past as it should have been lived can carry healing into the present. In the space of imagination where a person can go anywhere at any time, we go back to seek healing for Laura's early loss of her beloved father: Laura goes with her mother to the hospital, where her dying father holds her hand.*

*Laura asks her father the questions a child needs to ask. No, he is not leaving because she was a bad girl. No, he did not get sick because she was noisy. She is good. She is special. She is beloved.*

*Laura sits beside her father, reads him the story he asked her to write. It is about their trips to the mountain lakes, which she will always love because she knows she will find him there.*

*He looks at her with eyes that say he is blessed to know how she will remember him.*

*He holds her hands, tells her he loves her as deep and wide as the ocean and as high as the sky, just what he used to say at bedtime. She cries with him as he holds her in his arms. She tells him how much she loves him, will miss him. As she says goodbye, as she turns to go, Laura sees her father holding the little storybook she made for him to his heart.*

*In imagination, Laura goes to the funeral. She feels her mother's arm around her.*

*She holds her little brother's hand in hers. She feels the closeness of her family as they share their grief. She is not alone.*

*Now, tears flow. For the first time, Laura is crying the tears she could not cry as a child. Now it is the way it was supposed to be when she was a child. We are in a way blessed, for our emotional brains know nothing about past and present time. This part of our brain registers only experiences of wholeness in the now.*

*Laura has experienced this sense of wholeness in the creative and healing space of her imagination. For each of us, it is as it was for Laura: When we bring the painful things of our past into the place of wholeness, we release the past into the healing of the present moment. We create wholeness and healing and holiness, which knit new neural networks in our brains, in our hearts, in our very breathing.*

## Guided meditation: A ritual
## to unwind from old grief

BOTH THE CHILDREN OUTSIDE and the child inside need our loving attention when death arrives.

Come to your breathing—in and out, in and out.

Sense the door of your heart opening,

See the child within your heart who has been waiting for you to come after so long a time of being alone with an old, still-aching grief.

Know how your unwinding from this old grief will make it possible to be with your present loss in a more healing way.

In your meditation, look deeply into your child and see what grief he or she is still carrying from the past. Go back there with your child. See and sense the comfort that is needed by the child.

Take the time in your meditation to receive the guidance that will help you to help your child to live through this old loss, feeling the safety of being held by you and perhaps by others who he had wished were beside him in the past.

As you sit, quietly breathing, feel and know what was left incomplete for the child grief you suffered.

Perhaps the child wants its mother or father or sibling to come, as they were not able to then, to bring comfort, to hold the child. Let them come. See mother or father, or both, or someone needed come. Let completion happen.

Remember how, in this place of grief, there is no time.

There is only grief waiting for solace to come.

Perhaps your child self needs the completion of saying goodbye to loved one who just "disappeared."

Perhaps before your child self even knew what death was.

*Let whatever your child self needs to complete the mourning of the past happen.*

*Let your inner child know that no feeling need be hidden and frozen over.*

*Not anymore. Not ever again.*

*Your meditation time will help you breathe into and open your heart wide to the child within and to the children in your present life who need help with their loss and will help their feelings to flow freely in safety.*

*May you offer a shelter of presence for the grief that wants and needs to be held by you for the children around you and for the child within you.*

## *In your journal*

TITLE A NEW PAGE: "MY OLD GRIEF"

Is there a past loss that still lives in you, longing to receive healing in the present that it could not receive in the past? Perhaps because family members were too overwhelmed or because the child you were could not speak its needs. Let that loss know it is safe to appear now.

On one page, write the story of your old wounding grief. Allow your child self to tell the story. Give this story a title.

On a facing page, write the story of the way your child self would have given what it needed in its grief. From whom was comfort needed? Allow that person to appear and bring comfort to the child.

Allow to happen now what could not happen in the past. Perhaps it is a parent or a brother or sister who

in their deepest heart of hearts would have wanted to bring comfort to the child and who brings it now.

Give this story a title.

Title a new page: "My Present Grief"

Write the grief you are feeling for the loss of a loved one in your present life.

As you write under each title, be aware of how you are unwinding "then" and "now" in your memory.

Feel and sense and write what this means for your life and for you, fully honoring your past and present losses.

# 15.

## *I let go, I hold on, I let go*

WE OFTEN DEAL WITH THE INSECURITY of living in a world we cannot ultimately understand or control by trying to control ourselves and everything around us—our feelings, our time, our money, our children, our thoughts, our very lives. Then, just when we think we have everything under control and feel safe, death comes to us in all its fullness and unfathomable mystery, and, once again, we come face-to-face with the basic insecurity that is part of our living, showing us the inevitable limits of our control.

Death comes and shows us "change" is an unwavering law of life. Death is the great teacher, but there are smaller "deaths" constantly teaching us about loss and letting go: the loss of a job, of a love relationship, of our youth, of our health, of dreams we couldn't make come true.

Nothing can be held on to forever. Yet change does have its own laws and rhythms. We know the moon's phases are predictable, we watch seasons come and go in yearly cycles. Predictable rhythms abide in our lives. And then comes a shattering of our known universe: Children die young. Natural disasters bury cities in an instant. Bombs fall and destroy whole families while they are asleep in their beds. And too, for the most part, life has its seasons and cycles. When we let go into these natural turnings of all life, the insecurity and anxiety of existence can be held in something larger, something deeper, the predictable cycles of waxing and waning that move through all of creation, the continual cycles of change, which teach us that we are truly an in-between people, always passing from one stage of life to another. Life asking us to let go, to go on, to let go again and again, to go on again and again until our last breath.

*A young mother recently became pregnant with her third child. Helen had not planned for this pregnancy and was disappointed, as she had hoped to return to work when her youngest began nursery school. Nevertheless, she and her husband decided to have this child. In the third month of her pregnancy, Helen's mother, Sally, was diagnosed with stage-four lung cancer. She chose not to be treated and to let her illness and dying take its course. In the sixth month of Ellen's pregnancy, Sally entered hospice care.*

*As Helen and I sat together, she shared with me: "I sit with my mother every day. We sit in the quiet of the garden, her reclining on a lounge chair, me beside her. We hold hands, listen to the sounds of the birds. Sometimes my mother places her hand on my stomach, on the baby, and sings the same lullabies to this new being as she once sang to me.*

*Sometimes, I just want to hold on to her as tight as I can, never let her go. Just as I held on to her when I was a child, trying to make her stay and never leave me.*

*Sometimes she holds me tight, already missing me and the grand-*

*child she will never get to see.*

*I still become nauseated. I can't do anything right now but be with this pregnancy. I am aware I'm doing the same thing my mother dying in hospice is doing, being with what is inevitable. I do not really want this pregnancy, but because of my respect for this life, I accept it, just as my mother does not want her dying and is slowly coming to acceptance of it.*

*I cannot do anything about the nausea or about the pain in my back. The more I fight it, the worse it gets. And so, I let go, breathe into it. I will get bigger and bigger. Just like the moon. I will become full and heavy and filled with the light of new life. I sit with my dear mother and hold her hand and feel how she is pregnant with death.*

*There is a light that shines through her, the light of her being, more and more the pure essence of who she is.*

*Sometimes, we sit and smile at the light we see in one another. At other times, we sit and hold hands and tears come for the sadness of the loss that is happening. It is a kind of blessing that in this being together, we are learning to surrender to life's rhythms, me to life's coming and my mother to life's going."*

*Helen shows me a photograph taken by her husband of her and her mother. The light of love can be seen in each of them and between them. Tears come to each of us as we look at the photo.*

Letting go is a gradual process of widening into surrender, a gradual movement into acceptance and letting be. Letting go is a birthing process. We who stand beside our loved ones as they face their death are midwives easing their passage from one phase of life into the next. When it is our turn, letting go into our own dying will be a birthing process, one we prepare for as we are there for the dying of our loved ones.

## *Guided meditation: Holding on, letting go*

COME TO YOUR BREATHING, *slowly breathing in and breathing out.*

*Take three deep exhalations.*

*Count backward from three to two to one with each exhalation, and then count backward breathing out to zero.*

*See the zero become a golden circle.*

*See yourself standing in the center of the golden circle.*

*Step backward through the golden circle and find your self in a mountain meadow.*

*See how lovely the colors of the sky are, a pure golden sun and clear blue sky.*

*Breathe in the fresh and cleansing blue and gold and let the healing colors move through every cell of you.*

*Now, in this meadow, green with life, see yourself holding a beautiful kite.*

*Feel your hands loosen their hold as you begin to let the kite go.*

*Know the moment of not wanting to let go of this lovely kite—this loved one.*

*Allow the shifting from holding on to releasing.*

*Allow the back and forth rhythm from holding on to letting go, back and forth.*

*Let yourself know that it is time now for this kite, this beloved to be released.*

*Know how, as you release, it helps your loved one to be released into the vast blue heavens.*

*See yourself in a final letting go of the kite...sense your hands and heart releasing.*

*Watch the kite carried by the wind until it is beyond your sight.*

*Know how you are preparing and practicing for the letting go of your loved one.*

*Let yourself be breathed until you find yourself beside the loved one who is dying or who has already died. See yourself holding tight, crying out, "Do not go, you cannot go, you cannot fly away."*

*See yourself holding on. Feel the holding on in your body.*

*Now, let your body shift to letting go. Feel your whole body releasing.*

*Take one last deep exhalation and shift back to the scene of your not letting go, watching as you hold on even tighter.*

*Let these scenes move back and forth, just as your feelings move back and forth, swinging like the*

*pendulum of a clock, back and forth, from holding on tightly to releasing and letting go.*

*Know how you are in the natural human process of holding on and letting go of the one you love.*

*Know how holding on is the expression of your cherishing, your need to remain connected to this loved one.*

*See yourself holding even tighter, honoring your love, not ever wanting to let that love go.*

*Feel any movement of tears, even screams, to hold against the unbearable releasing of the one you love.*

*Breathe. . .stay with this back and forth movement, holding and releasing, until you see and feel even a small shift of easing into the movement of letting go of your loved one.*

*Watch what happens and sense how letting go of the person does not mean letting go of the love.*

*As you let go, sense and feel how the love between you will go on no matter what. It will always be there for you to hold and to be held by, softly, without grasping, always there to guide your heart along its way.*

*Feel and understand how your slow letting go is part of a deep and difficult process of coming to accept the natural and inevitable current of life and death as it moves through you like ocean waves, coming and going, forever coming and going.*

*Sense how you are a part of the great cosmic, organic flow of all life, moving through the phases of coming and going, life and death, holding on and letting go, until there is the letting be of all that is.*

*Sit and breathe and allow your heart to move softly with the awareness of how poignant this life and death are—this loving, this releasing, this letting go.*

## *In your journal*

OPEN YOUR JOURNAL TO TWO FACING PAGES.

On one page, write the title "I will never let you go."

On the facing page, write the title "I will find my way to let you go."

Choose the colors that reflect your voice for each state of feeling you need to express.

Take your time and write one feeling at a time on one side of the page and then on the other.

Keep writing without putting your colored pencil down.

Allow your feelings to flow onto the page.

If there are tears, allow your tears to do the writing and the same for any other feelings that want to flow out onto the page.

# 16.

## *I finish unfinished business*

FOR MONTHS AFTER MY FATHER DIED, *I received bill after bill from the funeral parlor for the death certificate they had provided. For months, I left these bills unopened on my desk. I can see now why I refused to finish this last bit of business: It would have brought a final closing to my father's death and funeral and I was not ready for "closure." The day I signed the six-dollar check and mailed it, I knew I had turned a corner. It was done: My father was dead and buried and the act of mailing that check helped me stand in this reality.*

Unfinished business is a constant reminder of our obligations in daily life: Unpaid bills, ignored correspondence, put-off phone calls nag us until we act. This happens in our spiritual life as well. When we have unfinished business with someone who has died, completion of the smallest obligations may seem impossible. Often, we hold on to unfinished business after a death in order to keep our hold on the past. Or we ignore a particular aspect of unfinished business because we can't imagine how to possibly complete it.

*When my father was dying, I stayed with him through the night and talked with him as he lost consciousness and began his journey out of his body. After he died, I left the hospital to make the arrangements for his funeral. My father died on a Thursday and since funerals are not held on the Sabbath in the Jewish religion, I needed to make a quick decision about his burial, so I arranged it for the following day.*

*Because I had to make my decision quickly, I did not do something considered essential to the burial of a Jewish man: I could not recover his prayer shawl in time for him to be buried in it. The prayer shawl is what a Jewish man wears throughout his life during his daily prayers from the time of his Bar Mitzvah at age 13, the ritual of his passage from being a boy to becoming a man. This prayer shawl is also what the man wears when he is buried. My father's prayer shawl was in the drawer of his dresser in another city and so I didn't have time to retrieve it for his burial.*

*I could not bring peace to my troubled heart because I had not honored my father as he would have hoped to be honored by this final rite of respect. This unfinished business stayed with me, calling me to do something more. A few months after my father's death, I asked my mother if I could have my father's prayer shawl. Perhaps I could complete unfinished business if I could have it in my keeping. My mother told me she had given it to my father's rabbi. When I visited the rabbi, he showed me the drawer where I could look through all the prayers shawls, but all of them looked alike, long, white with fringes and blue stripes. I left without even trying to find my father's, knowing I would never be able to identify it.*

*Shortly after my disappointing search for his prayer shawl, my father appeared to me in a dream, saying, "Prayer shawl is finished; my prayer shawl was finished with my life. You must make your own prayer shawl for your life now." I thought about the message of this dream throughout the year, pondering the mysterious instruction the dream brought to me: "What does it mean for me to make a prayer shawl for my own life?" At first, I thought the message meant I needed someone to help me create my own beautiful prayer shawl. But this didn't feel right or true. Slowly, in meditation, the answer unfolded: "Create your own prayer shawl in the form most meaningful to you, make it the embodiment of the essential love and goodness your parents and daughter and others have given you to carry through your life."*

*I now feel I am creating my own prayer shawl by writing this book and sharing the true fabric of my own journey and what I have learned while journeying with others.*

To make our own prayer shawl is to live our authentic being with gratitude to those who came before us, to honor the spiritual circle of our loved ones and of our ancestors reaching out to us and saying: "Thank you for taking on the difficult task of becoming a human being in your lifetime. We are grateful to you. What you do, you do for each of us as well. We are all One. And we are at peace."

Yes, we are called on to write the checks, send the letters, and make the phone calls that will bring the passing of our loved one to completion. We are also called upon to complete the deeper unfinished business our lives call out for. We are all linked with the living, with our beloved dead, and with our long-dead ancestors and to the force of life moving in us. We are called to live our lives authentically and to pay attention to the unfinished business that calls us to live from our true being.

## Guided meditation: My heart completes unfinished business

COME TO YOUR QUIET PLACE. *Sit with your breathing.*
*Place one hand on your stomach and the other upon your heart center.*

*Let your hands rise and fall with the rising and falling of your breath until you feel quiet and rest in the rhythm of your breath.*

*You may wish to play some meditative music.*

*Let the music calm you.*

*When you have come to calmness, ask yourself:*

*What unfinished business do I have around the death of my loved one?*

*Are there small tasks I have been avoiding, tasks in need of completion?*

*Is there, perhaps, something deeper calling for completion?*

*Perhaps you are sitting with regret over something you did or did not do before your loved one died. Perhaps an argument unresolved or a request not granted before it was too late.*

*Breath in and breathe out.*

*Perhaps there is unfinished business you long to complete for yourself, for your own grief, for going on in your life.*

*Perhaps there is unfinished business in relation to a family member around your loved one's dying and death.*

*Let yourself reflect in the quiet of your meditation on all that calls out for completion.*

*Know how your heart will find its way to peace through your devotion to completing small tasks and to listening and tending to what calls to you from deep within.*

*Breathe, listen as you write, be aware of listening to the whispers of your heart, letting you know what your life is longing for and what needs completion so that you can follow your sacred longings.*

## *In your journal*

GIVE YOURSELF THE SPACE AND TIME of stillness to sit with your journal beside you.

Write a commitment to the small things waiting to be tended to and completed so that they can be put to rest.

Listen in silence to your grief tell you what it longs for that remains unfinished.

Perhaps you heart calls you to tend to your grief in a particular way.

Perhaps to have a daily time of silence and solace perhaps to travel somewhere.

In your silence, listen until you hear.

After sitting with your questions, open your notebook and let your hand be moved by your heart.

Write what comes up for you regarding business that is calling to you for completion.

You may wish to write a letter to your loved one in your journal, expressing anything that asks for completion between the two of you.

Know how your writing creates healing and helps you complete unfinished business in the realm of spirit.

Perhaps there needs to be a conversation with a family member with whom unfinished business calls for completion. Perhaps you wish to write a letter to this person in your journal.

Unfinished business also calls for completion for those things in your heart that seek to find words of thanks and appreciation for those friends, family, and perhaps doctors, who brought you comfort throughout this process.

Write this unfinished business as well.

# 17.

## *Taking refuge*

THE TIME FOLLOWING THE LOSS OF A LOVED ONE is like no other. We are drawn to go through the door that opens onto the journey through the land of loss and love. As we find our way, the journey will slowly shape our grieving heart so that we become more deeply human and tender beings.

We often give up our grieving time because we are afraid to feel our feelings, afraid they will overwhelm us. We protect ourselves by rushing back into our busy lives, hoping our usual routines will shield us from the pain of loss. But, our grief does not go away, no matter how much we ignore it. Grief deferred goes into cold storage and waits there for as long it takes to begin a process of thawing frozen feelings so that they can be felt.

The land of loss in which we learn to bear our feelings is a space of transition, an in-between space, like a corridor, like the silence between two notes of music. It is an empty space between she-was-here and she-is-gone, he-was-here, he-is-gone. It is a space in which we meet the *no more* of our grief. We may feel terror, or a void, an endless desert, a bottomless dry well, a dark night with no hope of light.

*Sharon, an artist, spent the year after her husband died doing only the bare essentials of living: shopping, cooking, brushing her teeth, watching television. She spent long hours in empty silence, just sitting, staring into space, watching T.V. She told me she felt guilty for wasting time.*

*I told Sharon about a spiritual teacher who told his students he had thoroughly enjoyed his month-long retreat in the mountains of Canada. When asked what he had done, the teacher said, "Among other things, like long hours or meditation, I watched a lot of television."*

*He explained to his students how, as he looked at the television, he felt life deep within him gestating, ripening toward the surface of his awareness. He cooked and swept the floor with the same awareness, of allowing his deep self to gestate until it was ready to surface and bring fresh living to him.*

*To hear that an enlightened teacher watched television gave Sharon permission to do mindless things without guilt. Without guilt, she lay dormant in the in-between spaces of her grief. In time, on some days, Sharon could sense that while, on the surface of her being, she simply stared at the television screen, cooked her meals, and in a muted way did daily chores, within the ground of her deep self, quiet stirrings were felt as they birthed shoots of new life.*

*As the first year of her mourning came to a close, Sharon gradually found herself more interested in living, felt sap rising in her being. She began going for slow walks, going out to dinner, enjoying visits with family. She began to draw and paint the shades of her grief journey. Sharon's self-acceptance to simply "be," to do "nothing," allowed her deep wise self to arise and guide her through the empty, aching feelings of the in-between spaces.*

*One day, Sharon dreamed of visiting her husband's grave. She found a single purple flower growing upon the mound. Purple is Sharon's favorite color and she took the flower to be a gift of new life from*

*her husband, affirming and blessing the sense of aliveness she was be-*
*ginning to feel rising in the fallow places of her body and spirit.*

Sharon watched television. You will find your own way to be fallow in the empty, waiting spaces.

There is no better way to live in the empty spaces. Each one of us finds
our own way along the in-between spaces of this difficult path. What matters
is for you to sense, even in a small corner of your being, that what feels like
"dead space" may well be a space of hidden faith in being born anew.

I have been comforted in the in-between time of grief by being
where nature can soothe me; where I can aimlessly walk long stretches
by myself; find a space to stop, sit, cry, write in my journal; rest on the
grass looking into the vast sky. Comfort also comes from close friends,
who I can call to sit or walk with me. It is this balance of being in the
empty, in-between spaces and returning to the islands of human comfort that gets me through.

The in-between spaces of the grief process are different for each of
us. There are those who want to be at home, where the ordinary things
bring comfort: making a cup of tea, sipping it while sitting quietly,
working alone in the garden, touching the earth, pulling weeds, tending
life, making a quiet dinner, or making no dinner at all. Being close to
the space shared with the person who is there no more. Feeling the
empty space. Being touched by the silence, by the echoes, by the finality. Not believing it. "She must be coming back." No. And silence
again. Touched by the stark nakedness of loss. All to be felt.

All to be lived with. Time for the sorrow, the bewilderment, the
terror, the painful ache, the loving memories.

Time also to sit with close ones, to take comfort in knowing this is *the
time* to share feelings of relief that the suffering is over, to laugh and cry while
remembering the blessings and the trials. *Time* to walk through rooms and
touch things that belonged to *someone* and now belong to *no one.*

In the in-between spaces of loss and love, may you accept feeling lost. As you realize you don't know what to do next, may you let yourself be who you are now, may you trust something will come from your deep self, from somewhere, to show you your next step. May you be touched by the quiet stirrings of hidden life. May you trust in the mystery of the unseen as it begins to stir in the spaces of your grief.

## Guided meditation: Taking refuge at the crossroad of life and death

COME TO YOUR BREATHING. *As you inhale, feel your breath rising with the whole soft front of your body.*

*As you exhale, feel your breath releasing.*

*Now, come to stillness. Be aware of the space between your exhale and your inhale, between your last breath out and your next breath in.*

*Let yourself feel this in-between space between your breaths.*

*Be aware of not knowing when your next breath will come, but it always does—until your last breath.*

*Allow yourself to rest in this waiting space between breaths.*

*As you breathe, consider how faith and trust are built into every breath you take: You will breathe in, you will breathe out and in-between your breaths, there is a quiet space, empty, and then the next breath comes.*

*In the same way, as you sit in the in-between spaces of grief, know this as a place and time where you wait for signs of life to come and touch you again. Be in touch with the waiting space, where there is nothing to do but witness your living now in an in-between space.*

*In the olden days, when someone wandered on a pilgrimage, they would come to a fork in the road and would not know which path to take.*

*It was not time to know the next step, not time to go on.*

*Know how now you are such a pilgrim on your journey in the land of grief.*

*Know how it is your time to be in-between what was before and what is yet to come.*

*Like the pilgrim of old, see a small hut in which you can stay until you sense which way to go.*

*Enter this place of solace and waiting, this place to be in as you journey along the way of your loss.*

*See what is in this place: perhaps a table and chair, a simple bed.*

*Perhaps a journal on your table. Perhaps a pitcher of clear, living water from a nearby well.*

*Look and see.*

*Know this to be your place until your next steps along the path are revealed to you.*

*You can always come to this place in your meditation.*

*Spend as much time as you wish in this refuge place.*

*Know you have all the time you need to be here. Accept that there can be no rushing.*

*Breathe in and breathe out. Be aware of the space between your breaths.*

*Wait for and witness the next breath as it comes.*

*Ask yourself: What do I truly need in this place of refuge during this in-between time of my life, this time between my known past and my unknown future?*

*May your refuge help you know an inner place of comfort.*

*May you be surprised when a new breath comes to call you onto the path of life.*

## *In your journal*

FEEL AND KNOW HOW IT IS YOUR TIME now to dwell in in-between space.

Simply being, breathing, becoming quiet.

Listening into the quiet, waiting in the empty space until you hear.

During this time, out of the silence within you, you may begin to speak, not to another person, but into the silence surrounding you.

You may speak whatever sits inside of you. Remember, your tears speak too.

Listen to them speak out of their silence to be heard by you.

Let yourself speak, and then become silent. Listen into the silence. Does a voice come out of the silence to speak to you, to touch you from somewhere unseen?

As you listen and hear, let your hand reach for your pen to write.

Or reach for your colored pencils and draw what you receive in your in between space.

Know how sacred this space is, how desert emptiness can turn to an unexpected sense of green, of something stirring, growing, calling you.

Perhaps what you receive out of the silence is without color, is the aloneness of gray, the despair of black.

Let it all speak onto the open page of your journal, with words, with color and shape.

And then allow the silence of your in between self to return. Be there. Wait there.

Does anything else stir, a next breath of life breathing you, calling you?

If so, take the time to write.

# 18.

## *Letting go of belongings left behind*

THE BELONGINGS LEFT BEHIND BY A LOVED ONE bear both life and loss. They surround us with vivid memory and aching loss. They stand empty, without their owner, and reflect the emptiness we feel, bereft of the living presence of our loved one.

We are like these objects, alone, uprooted, disconnected, waiting for a time when we will know where we belong, where we will put down new roots, not knowing if we ever will. Meanwhile, we are suspended in in-between space, just like the clothing, the books, the toothbrush, the chair left empty at the table—the shawl, bathrobe, slippers, coffee cup, and so much more.

The process of dealing with what remains behind takes on great meaning for us. As we let go of the things containing the life energies of our loved one, we are tangibly letting go of the person. Some of us let go of everything quickly, give everything to the Salvation Army so that we do not have face the feelings likely to surface with the decisions of what to keep, what to let go.

Whenever possible, it is ultimately healing for us to go through the belongings ourselves. Although it may be wrenching at first, you may find healing in touching and sorting what belongs to the past and what to take along into your future. In this in-between time, you may find a sort of solace, even if it takes you days, weeks, or months to accomplish this sorting.

*Laura wants to sort through the clothing and hats her mother made. She knows she will need time to sit with the clothes that hold so much of her mother within them. She waits several months until she is ready.*

*With her daughters at her side, she sorts slowly through the clothing, deciding what to do with these treasured objects. Laura feels her mother's life as she holds these possessions. Memories sweep over her. She weeps over this hat, that dress, what to take with her, what to leave behind, what her daughters wish to have. Sometimes she laughs through her tears while reminiscing about special moments stitched into this dress, that hat. As she touches each piece, Laura is saying goodbye to her mother and, at the same time, embracing her living. This is a sorting ritual of touching and cherishing the life and memories of her mother while releasing her mother's physical presence.*

You may find yourself choosing to hold on to some things that have special meaning for you. You may surround yourself with the comfort of these things now and find yourself letting go of them as time goes by. We need time to take our comfort and sort our emotions that are wrapped in our loved one's possessions. We need both the rhythm of comfort as we hold and behold what is left behind and the rhythm of sorting and releasing.

Over time, we may find there is just one thing we want to keep, just one object that becomes a symbol connecting us to our loved one. For me, it is my daughter's little red rattan chair. It stands in a corner of the room where little children love to sit when they come to visit.

I kept my father's silver dollar, the one he carried in his pants pocket for good luck since the Depression days. Every day, I use the blue and white dishes I gave my mother when I was a teenager. I drink my tea from the cup my friend Nina made for me—brown with a yellow flower and a broken handle. All their other things have dropped away, some living on in memory, others fallen into oblivion.

Some things may take a very long time to let go of. My daughter's yellow toothbrush stayed in the toothbrush holder for more years than I want to admit. Soon after 9/11, I thought of how many parents would stand and stare at their son's or daughter's toothbrush, stand there swallowed by that awful chasm of stunned silence. In honor of and in communion with these mothers and fathers, I let go of Leslie's toothbrush. Letting go of that took an afternoon of being home alone, feeling the old ache reawaken in my chest, shedding fresh tears, and then quietly wrapping the little yellow toothbrush in an old lace handkerchief, kissing it and placing it into a box of old things to be picked up as trash.

While you sort the belongings of your loved one, may you be blessed with having the time to treasure the life you are holding and the life you are releasing.

May you hold the intention to let life flow and take its course both for your loved one and your self.

## *Guided meditation: Releasing my loved one's belongings*

*ALLOW THE PROCESS OF LETTING GO of your loved one's possessions become a meditation in which the inner quiet you find may help you to receive guidance for your decisions.*

*As you sit quietly, imagine yourself sorting through the belongings your loved one has left behind.*

*What would give you the greatest comfort in this process?*

*Do you wish to do this alone? Do you wish help from family, friends?*

*Who can best help you sort through your emotions as well as the physical things?*

*Who can best help you make decisions; listen to your stories; help you decide what to hold on to, what to let go of, who might want this, or treasure that?*

*In your quiet space, sense and see who is there with you.*

*Feel and sense a person, a couple of people, or a circle of presence, supporting and comforting you.*

*Know you can create this for yourself.*

*When would it feel right for you to begin the process of sorting your loved one's belongings?*

*Consider the right timing to enter this sacred process.*

*Perhaps there are belongings you know you able let go of now. Allow yourself to let go of things that did not hold meaning to your loved one and are no longer needed.*

*In this clearing out, know how you are sifting and sorting belongings that did matter to your loved one and may matter to you and letting go of those that did not.*

*Understand how, as you release one physical thing at a time, you are also releasing the physical presence of the one who has left.*

*Sense the letting go. As you exhale, breathe, releasing not just your breath but belongings that lived with you and your loved one as well.*

*Allow any feelings that come, of sadness, of precious memories, of peace tied to these belongings as you release them.*

*Let yourself sense how, as you sort their belongings, your loved one is being released, unwinding little*

*by little, into the great peace and light beyond all material form.*

*And because you remain connected to physical form, allow yourself to choose those belongings that you want to live on with you. Perhaps a favorite chair he loved to sit in, perhaps an afghan she covered herself with, perhaps cherished music he loved to listen to. Give yourself time to sit with and sort through belongings that are treasured.*

*Let yourself feel the deep warmth of connection that the objects you keep provide for you. And, at the same time, let yourself feel the bond between you and your loved one that abides beyond any physical belongings.*

## *In your journal*

PERHAPS THERE IS SOMETHING that belonged to your loved one that is especially hard to let go of.

Something holding special memory: perhaps a piece of jewelry, a coffee cup, a pair of slippers, a sweater, a toothbrush. Something you are aware of grasping tightly because you feel it keeps your loved one alive for you.

If it feels right for you, let yourself sit with this object in your space of solace. Be with it. Speak with it.

Let it speak to you. Know what of your life with your loved one is wrapped within this object. Write.

Tell this object the difficulty you are having in releasing it because it holds so much of your loved one.

Tell it how you also want to release it because, in some part of your heart, you are ready to let go of the holding on to an object, as if without it, you will no longer feel close to your loved one. Be aware of how you want to free yourself and your loved one of holding them tight. Let yourself be with the tears that come as you reach another and yet another layer of letting go. Give yourself time to write.

As you sit quietly with this object, perhaps you will hear your beloved's voice speak through the object and guide you. Perhaps you can ask your loved one's spirit to help you know what to do. Is there someone who would be grateful to be blessed with its presence? Someone you would like to pass this object on to?

In the quiet, allow your body to feel the rhythm of holding, of releasing.

Be aware of what part of your body is unwinding, and what part is holding fast to your loved one with the help of this object.

Breathe into your heart. Sit in silence. Reflect on how you may go on with this object while knowing that it holds precious connection. At the same time, feel deep into your heart where your love lives without any need of a material symbol. Let yourself know the difference.

Look within your body, your heart, and your memories and sense if you are able to carry what is wrapped in this object without carrying the object. When you can feel how you carry your beloved in your heart without any outer symbol, know that you are truly free to choose to carry this special object as a talisman of your connection.

Write about that which you release and of that which always remains yours to have and hold of your loved one.

If it is not yet time to let go of this object, perhaps you might write a letter to the object itself.

Something like, "Dear toothbrush, I am not ready to let you go yet. I need to see you every day, to remember the mornings and the nights of my loved one using you. It will take time. One day, I will be ready to let you go. One day."

# 19.

## *Numb*

HOW IS IT POSSIBLE EVERYTHING AROUND ME looks the same, when I know nothing will ever be the same again? Everything seems to be in its fixed position. The clock is still ticking. The geranium on the windowsill is still a brilliant red. Morning still comes, and so does night. How can everything still be the same when the whole universe seems to have shifted? My eyes squint and my brow furrows as I try to understand. But this death, this absence, cannot be understood. It is beyond all understanding.

Bewilderment and numbness enfold you in the feeling of no feeling.

This numbness protects you from things you cannot understand, from things that are too painful, too much to bear. Like needing to shield your eyes from a naked, blinding sun, you cannot behold death and loss without some protection. For most of us, this protection is our illusion that our life and the lives of those we love will keep going on. Now, in the land of grief, we are looking at the sun without any shield. There are no sunglasses. We are left with only our numbness to shield us until we grow more accustomed to the glare of the reality of our blinding loss.

Numbness is a kind of mercy. Numbing protects you from feelings too powerful to bear, filters your feelings, allows them to come through to you slowly so you can tolerate the pain. It is like an emotional, digestive process. During the days immediately following loss, during the days and weeks and months to come, opportunities will arise for you to begin to feel what is just under the numbness.

You may notice that your hand has a life of its own, coming to rest on your chest or softly stroking your arm, tenderly soothing those feelings just below the thin ice of protection. When you are ready, you may take the time to feel just below the numbness, to come to be with your numbness, to sense it. Not to change your numbness, just to be with it, with tender touch.

In the numbness of grief, there may be a sense that you too, have departed, are no longer alive. There may be a feeling of deadness, of no feeling, of not being. When your world is no longer the same, when the familiar presence of a loved one has vanished, the *me* you have known in relation to *the other* feels a no-moreness. You may feel that "a part of me has gone with him," or "Without her, I do not know where to place my next step. I am left here alone, stripped, with no mooring, no compass. No up. No down. No feeling."

Without the one who has died, the ground beneath you becomes less firm. It takes time on this journey of grief to find footing. Your vision may feel unfocused, your feet unsteady, the world a blur. You may literally lose your way while driving, not knowing where you are on a familiar route, have to stop and re-orient. During this in-between period, friends and family members are our familiar landmarks, our rock, a cairn along the road so we do not become totally lost. To see and be seen by them, to touch them and be touched by them, brings the touchstone of human contact that we so need.

You may want to find a balanced rhythm of company and quietness. Company so that you are not alone, quietness because you are alone and yet not alone, for you can sense the safety net of relationship nearby, embracing you even in your solitude.

Being alone need not be the same as loneliness. Being alone can be a time of coming to your self, sensing your numbness slowly and gently lifting, as an anesthesia begins to wear off after protecting us with its no-feeling. The wisdom of your psyche will know when to slowly lift the numbness it has wound you in to protect you from a "too muchness" of grief. Ever so slowly, through the layers of frozen loss, you begin to feel the safety of your rhythm of aliveness.

*Eve sits at night knitting and listening to music after everyone is asleep. As she knits, she lets her heart follow the rhythm of the knitting needles. Then, she puts them down, becomes quiet and listens to the rhythm of her heart, of the deep sorrow for the loss of her husband, for the father of her children. She begins to feel the sadness, the missing, the longing move through her numbness.*

*During the day, Eve must be an adult, a mother to her children. In the quiet, after everyone is asleep, she touches her feelings just below the numbness. She breathes into her fear of aloneness in the pit of her stomach. She places her hands there, gives comfort to the clutch of fear, helps it to calm. On some nights, Eve sobs, feeling the pain in her heart, letting grief flow. After a while, she feels her breathing become more regular, quieter. Slowly, she finds her way to the soft holding rhythm of her breathing.*

Eve is slowly coming to a sense of protection other than numbing, one that allows her to be in touch with what sits in her as real. Alive is not just to feel happy. Sadness and fear and longing are aliveness as well. When we find the courage and capacity on the path of our grief to receive the flow of what comes, we are likely to feel what can be called "peaceable," a sense of being authentically present for all that arises within us through our numbness, to all of our authentic self, to all the myriad colors of being alive.

## Guided meditation: Touching my numbness

*Come to your place of solitude, sitting or lying down.*

*Make yourself comfortable, loosening anything tight so that you can breathe without outer constriction.*

*Allow your breathing to take you to where in your body you may feel the numb place of your grief.*

*Place your hand upon that place in your body where you have tuned into a numbing of feeling, a dead place, empty and frozen. Perhaps your hand will place itself on your heart. . .or your solar plexus. . .upon your stomach. . .or your face. . .your jaw. . .your neck. . .over your eyes.*

*As you touch the place of numbness, let your hands feel the numbness as made of some material, a physical shield having form that covers over your feelings.*

*What is the shield made of? Velvet, metal, ice, a steel-clutching hand. . .what?*

*Hear the sounds or simply the pulsing of something that sits just below the shield.*

*Take the time to listen quietly for what may want to speak or sound through your numbness, even the sound of no sound perhaps the sound of hollow emptiness.*

*Where and what do you touch? What do you feel? What*

*do you hear? What do you feel and sense?*

*Even though you are a grown woman, a grown man, a mother, a father, in this quietness, you may feel or hear, just below the numbness, wrapped up in it, how frightened and alone you are without your loved one's presence.*

*You may touch a sense of guilt or sorrow that you were not all you wished to be with your loved one during the dying process, or while the two of you were healthy and living your lives together.*

*Or perhaps you touch a sense of terror beneath the numbness? The terror of not knowing what will become of your life.*

*Or feel a regret that it is too late now, with your loved one gone, to make things right.*

*Listen to your feelings below the numbness. Be with your numbing of "I have no-feelings."*

*Let yourself be with whatever wants to be heard, just under where your hand touches.*

*Can you bring the presence of your breath to this numb place, carry compassion there with your touch with your breath?*

*If it is time, allow yourself to be, to feel, just a bit less numb, a bit more sensing your aliveness of the feelings there.*

*Can you hear or see into your numbness, into what is just under it, at the very center of it?*

*Listen quietly, slowly breathe acceptance into whatever is there, letting your authentic self be in this moment. Accept that numbness may be authentically you at this time.*

*Let the numbness itself and what is just below it feel your hand, your touch, and your acceptance.*

*Can your hand reach beneath layers of numbness to where*

*some feelings stir?*

*If not, if you feel nothing, hear nothing, know how this shield of numbness is protecting you from what it fears you are not ready to feel.*

*Feel your gratitude for this shield and how it will go on protecting you until you are ready to let it know you can let it soften.*

*If it is time to feel into your numbness, place your hand on it and let it know, "I am ready to feel what you are protecting me from feeling. You can open now and come to me. I will call for your protection if and when I am in need of it. Thank you for taking care of me. Now I have the protection of my sense of compassion that can touch and be with the pain of my loss."*

## *In your journal*

Draw your image of what it is that protects you with its numbing. What does it look like?

Listen to how it speaks to you as your protector and tells how it protects you and from what. Write what you hear.

If is time for your numbness to soften, let it know with the tender touch of your hand that it can. Let the numb place feel the strength of your hand and of how you are ready to come to your feelings.

Write the feelings that open as softening happens.

See and sense what touches the softened place. Perhaps a hand of compassion? Perhaps a sound.

Perhaps the presence of your loved one.

Write or draw, or both, all that you sense and see and feel in this softening of your numbness.

# 20.

# *The circle of consolation*

THE ONE CLOSE AND DEAR HAS DIED. His or her physical presence is gone. A cut has taken place in the bond that connected the two of you, as surely as if it were a physical cut. You may actually feel the pain of loss as a physical cut in your chest, solar plexus, or stomach.

In the Jewish tradition, the first thing the mourner does upon hearing that someone has died, is to rip the garment of whatever clothing she is wearing. The sudden sound of the tearing echoes the tearing of the heart and the tearing of the fabric of the mourner's life. Even though we know that the bond of the spirit can never be cut, the cut at the physical level can be an excruciating hurting. With this tearing, you enter the land of grief, the country called loss.

In this time of being severed from the cord of life that joins living to living, you may feel more acutely than ever a sense of stark aloneness. You may feel like a motherless child, like a childless mother, like a husbandless wife—as if a part of yourself has been amputated. At this time, when we feel small and stunned and bereft, it is the instinct of those who go on living and loving you to gather around and enfold you in their comfort. They gather around you to kindle light and warmth in the sudden winter that has encircled your soul.

After the funeral, this instinct to console the one who is mourning often finds expression in the circle of consolation, during which the mourner sits at home with closest family members and receives visitors.

This time can be one of great comfort.

You do not have to join in the talk if you don't feel like it. Just sitting quietly with those around you can bring comfort. Visitors do not even need to say hello to you when they enter the house, so as not to burden you with reciprocating so much as the return of a greeting.

Feel free to sit in silence, to speak when you feel like it, to ask for food or drink when you need it. This is not a time to worry about being polite to people. What matters most now, what will be most healing, is that you and they be very tender to your needs. You may wish to take some quiet time in your room, to ask someone to sit with you, perhaps hold your hand, to serve you some food or drink. You may wish to ask someone to sit and meditate or pray with you, or sing you a song of solace, or sit with you in a holding silence.

Know the consolation you require at this very vulnerable time and allow yourself to receive it. The word "console" means "to comfort together." This is truly a time to comfort together, to be aware of one another's perhaps differing needs for solace. If others in the family sit in mourning alongside you, know how unforgettable it shall be if you feel from one another the tender caring for each other's needs.

What more can we do in the face of loss than to affirm the presence of the bond of comfort among the living, to feel the gratitude of having our needs seen and met and to honor those of the others in our circle? Some needs for solace will not be able to be met but what matters is that each person feel his longing being seen. How else to bless life in the face of death?

In the circle of consolation, you may wish to share precious photographs and tell stories of your life with the one who has died. You may wish to talk of the good times and the bad, to share both blessings and regrets. You may wish to include the little ones in the circle so that they, too, may listen and share and remember and feel consoled.

May you know how to create your circle of consolation so that it can hold silent comfort as well as the inner space from which to hear and speak the feelings that sit in the heart.

## Guided meditation: Entering the garden of comfort

*When the circle of family and friends has drawn to a close and the consolation of that circle is no longer around you and you miss the presence of its comfort, this meditation waits for you.*

*When you awake, before entering the activities of the day, take some time to be alone.*

*Sit or lie down quietly in your place of comfort.*

*Be with your breathing for a while, breathing in and breathing out, resting in the pause between breaths.*

*Wait until the next breath comes to you.*

*Be with the rhythm of your breathing. Let yourself be breathed.*

*Ask yourself: What shall be my comfort today? With whom do I want to spend some healing time? Do*

*I need alone time? Do I need both? Is there somewhere I want to be that will surround me with comfort?*

*As you breathe, let yourself listen until you hear.*

*Perhaps you want to connect with a person who is a consoling presence for you. Perhaps that person is not near, but you can let them come to you in the space and time of imagination.*

*Perhaps you cannot go to the place of comfort where you wish to be.*

*Still, you can be there in the space and time of imagination.*

*If you wish to be guided to a place of comfort, as you breathe, find your way to a spring meadow, green with life. Be aware of the scent of roses carried to you by a gentle breeze. Follow the scent until you come to a quiet rose garden. Breathe and enter the garden. Sense how the rose garden is filled with a silence as peaceful as the silence at the very center of each rose in the garden.*

*Breathe in the scent of the silence of the roses and of the peace pulsating all around you.*

*Be aware of the light of the time of day.*

*Look around until you see a bench See someone sitting there waiting to bring you comfort.*

*See who sits there waiting for you. Sit with the person. Is this person someone you know? Are you surprised to see who appears?*

*Be aware of the presence of loving comfort this person on the bench brings to you. Sense how the person's face sees your face, how their eyes touch you with deep seeing from their heart. Feel how they see and know your grief.*

*Let yourself know how this person is the gardener of the garden of comfort.*

*Be in the garden of comfort for as long as you wish.*

*When it is time to go, thank the one who will always be there to bring you comfort.*

*Just as you leave the garden, see the gardener approach you and whisper something into your left ear.*

*Hear what has been whispered and know that this word or these words are for your comfort as you continue along the path of your grief.*

*See yourself leaving the garden. Walk through the meadow and return to your seat.*

*Carry the comfort and scent of consolation within you. Carry the words whispered to you.*

*Carry a drop of silence from the center of the rose. Carry all of it in the center of your heart.*

*Know you can always return to your garden. All you need to do is enter your space of quiet, come to your breathing, cross the meadow, and enter your garden. Find the bench and the one who waits for you.*

## *In your journal*

Write your meditation into your journal. While writing, take your time to sit with the comfort you received. You may pause every now and then to breathe the sense of comfort.

Write the words you heard whispered into your ear onto their own page.

Do you wish to ask the one who is tends your garden any questions or share any feelings? Take the time to write them and listen to the responses given to you.

If you wish, you can take the meditative time to draw you garden of comfort.

You may linger over the scent of the roses.

You may breathe with the silence at the center of each rose.

You may find a rose in your heart, carrying a sacred silence.

As you do so, let yourself know how your heart is like the rose, holding sacred silence at its center.

# 21.

## *I live through the long nights*

IT IS NIGHT. Everyone in the house is asleep. Or, if you live alone, everyone you know out there is beyond your reach. Only silence surrounds you, silence and the dark night. You may hear an occasional car go by, an occasional creaking sound, a dog barking, someone stirring, somewhere. And then silence again. The silence may seem endless, the night endless, your grief unbearably endless.

In this silence, in the absence of all distraction, the pain of grief often opens wide. There seems to be no promise of comfort or contact. You realize how even the mere passing physical presence of others is, in itself, a comfort: the storekeeper who says hello, the friendly bus driver who nods to you, the person standing next to you as you wait for the green light. The comfort of human presence sustains and anchors us in the flow of life. But where is your comfort now, in this long night?

In the night, when someone has gone away, never to return, your aloneness and the pain of your loss can seem so vast that you will never get through to morning. When people were with you earlier in the day, you may have felt a wish to be alone with your sorrow, but now that you are alone, you may long for people to be near you. You wonder if morning will ever return. It does not matter whether you live with others or alone, for in grief it is alone that each of us go through the nights. It is alone we must each confront our loss. It is alone we begin to reckon with the ultimate reality of loss and impermanence and of our essential existential aloneness.

And yet, over time, somehow, through the depths of your aloneness, you may discover paths of solace you never knew before. Simply getting up to make a cup of tea may comfort you. Simply holding the warmth of the cup as you sit in the silence after a long time of tossing and turning in bed may calm you.

Simply holding a cup of tea—breathing in and out, sipping, tears, silence, sipping—may bring solace.

A cup of tea can become a warm companion on a long, dark night. Sitting, drinking, walking about, sitting again, waiting for the first light of dawn, slowly we are learning how to be with the aloneness of our sorrow, listen to the needs of our hurting self, placing a hand on those needs as they call to us in our body.

As we move through the long nights of being alone, we come to allow tears to move, allow the heart to feel as mute, as endlessly dark as the night and discover how we somehow survive dark and aloneness and broken places in our soul. We find we not only survive. Somehow, we find some capacity within to carry it all, a capacity that until now, we did not know we had. This capacity to hold what is most difficult for us births a sense of compassion in us. We discover and treasure how, through the deepest darkness, the light flickers and a bird sings the coming of morning into our broken heart.

*Grace and Harold have had a good marriage and are looking for-*
*ward to his retirement, saving to fulfill the long-time dream of travel*
*through Europe. Then Harold gets colon cancer and they must use*
*their savings for medical treatments.*

*When Harold dies, Grace is left with broken dreams, bereft of the*
*husband she loves and bereft of the wonderful future they had envi-*
*sioned. She never imagined living without him, missing out on their*
*long-planned retirement and growing old together.*

*Grace's nights are hardest. She thinks of committing suicide. She*
*cannot imagine getting through her grief, of going on without Harold.*
*For nearly a year, she stays awake at night and naps during the day.*
*Slowly, Ellen begins to write in her journal during the long nights. She*
*lights a candle and writes her memories as they appear to her out of*
*the dark silence. Slowly, she realizes she is recording for her grand-*
*children. She begins to include photos in the book. She tells tales of*
*the joys and struggles she and Harold shared. She writes poems. She*
*wants these youngsters to know the lives of their grandparents, to have*
*a legacy of her and Harold that will continue on after them.*

*Out of the anguished nights comes a beautiful tribute to her life*
*with her husband, a beautiful gift to her grandchildren and great grand-*
*children. Looking into and recording the past becomes a deeply healing*
*and spiritual nighttime ritual for Grace.*

Out of the dark nights, our soul slowly gives birth to something
new. We do not know how this unfolding happens. We only sense
being touched by the healing that grows as sorrow opens to be held in
solitude. We learn that, in darkness, a new part of us can grow, a new,
quiet center can be created, an inner home. We may even call this
center our true home, a hard-earned inner place. Perhaps it is coming
to know the abiding of this center, born in our darkness that we can
call "faith." In solitude, a new light is kindled. It is a mystery how this

light comes into our darkness, a light so tender, so poignant, more precious than any other. With this new inner light, we tenderly embrace the darkness, in ourselves and in others. This light is the tender light of mercy that comes to find us in the long night.

## Guided meditation: Comfort in the long night

*As you sit quietly, ask yourself: What will be my comfort through the nights which seem never to end?*

*Take time during the day to reflect on how you will get through the coming night.*

*Take your time to feel into this question.*

*You may wish to reach out to a friend before it gets too late, before the long night begins.*

*You may wish to share your night plans and feelings with this person.*

*You may find comfort while listening to soothing music that touches your soul as you prepare for the night and even during the night.*

*Write in your journal: It is a good friend always there, waiting for you.*

*Brew a pot of tea. Use your special cup that is a warm comfort to hold.*

*Take up your knitting or crochet, be with the rhythm of your knitting, let it comfort you.*

*Gather photos of you and your loved one into an album and write the stories that belong with them.*

*Create a legacy of your life and relationship with your loved one to share with family and friends.*

*These are just some of the evening rituals that you may turn to for comfort and meaning.*

*You may turn toward your evening rituals and find solace in their predictable nightly rhythm.*

*If you are having trouble sleeping during the night, a practice of deep breathing may help to calm your nervous system.*

*With one hand on your belly and one on your chest, breathe slowly in for four breaths, hold for seven breaths, then breathe out for six or eight. Use whatever number gives your breathing ease; breathe slowly without effort*

*You can simply breathe in and out and talk to yourself as you breathe: "My neck is relaxing, my eyes are relaxing, my jaw is letting go, my chest is loosening, my belly is softening, my tongue is resting in my mouth. Tears are coming; tears are moving through me; tears are going; tears are coming. Waves and waves of tears coming and going. I allow them."*

*As you breathe in and breathe out, a word or words of solace may come on your breath.*

*Perhaps: sacred, tears, peace, quiet, love, forever, alone, sad.*

*What is your word that whispers comfort as you breathe?*

*You may sit, or lay in bed, quietly breathing. Tears may come.*

*If there is deep sobbing, listen until the sobs take on a rhythm, moving as waves in the ocean, in and out, in and out.*

*Know how you are being held in the comfort of the rhythm of the waves.*

*If the nights are too difficult to get through, hopefully you will seek the help of your clergy, a bereavement counselor, or your circle of support.*

*With help and comfort, may you find your way to solace in the night.*

*May a seed of healing strength grow in you as you slowly, very slowly, find your way in the night.*

*May the sense of endless night begin in time to turn toward the quiet peace of the solitude of your heart.*

## *In your journal*

As you prepare for being alone in the night, perhaps after dinner, you may wish to write in your journal what will bring you comfort in the night.

As you write your intention for the evening, know how you are beginning to call forth the comfort that will come to you during the night.

You may sit holding a warm drink in your hands, you may slowly look at photographs you have set out before you. . . sipping your drink. . .gazing at the photos. . .

Let what comes to you as you breathe quietly. . .if tears, let tears write on the blank page. If regret, let regret write . . . Sense and feel how, in the quiet of the night, your feelings can find a refuge to be sat with. . .

Give any feeling that arises the space and time of the quiet night to write.

In the quiet of the night, you may sit or lay down under the comfort of a blanket. You may drift and enter a waking dream space. Be there as long as you need to be. Then, write your waking dream into your journal. Be aware of what your dream might be bringing you or trying to tell you. Write your dream into your journal.

If you wish, draw the images that came in your waking dream.

# 22.

## *I turn guilt to regret*

BILL'S MOTHER DIED FIVE YEARS AGO. He still feels guilty that he did not love her more when she was alive. Linda feels guilty that she did not allow her son, who died of leukemia at age 18, to drive across the country with friends after his high school graduation. She thinks often that she deprived him of a last, joyous experience.

*Jane, afraid of the wires and tubes he was attached to, did not reach to touch her husband's hand at the time of his death. She feels guilty. Guilt is at the core of her regret. Fear cut off her loving instinct. Behind her guilt, her regret says, "We went through so much together, for better and for worse. I wanted us to go through those last moments in the best way." Her regret has turned to guilt because her husband has gone and there is no longer a tomorrow in which to take hold of his hand, to do what she feels she should have done.*

Guilt arises when we fall short of creating the goodness and the fullness of love we long to give and receive in our relationships. At bottom, guilt springs from our truest self and expresses our sacred longing to be fully alive and connected. There is an inner spark of life that propels us to become the most we can be, to be our best selves, to live from the deepest core of our being and to express that in our daily deeds. But we can only try to come close to our vision. We will always fall short, for we are flawed humans. We are all here only learning how to love, never getting it perfect.

I have yet to meet a person who does not live with some sense of guilt for something he wishes he had been or done or had not been or had not done at the close of a loved one's life. Wrapped in almost everyone's guilt is the regret not to have been all that they could have been. We know we are not perfect, but we long to be true to ourselves and true to those we love.

There are three kinds of guilt: false guilt, true guilt, and unrelenting guilt.

False guilt comes from failing to live up to outer expectations. This guilt belongs to the messages we received in childhood about how to be a "good person," how to be accepted and admired. When false guilt becomes severe, its self-punishment can cripple and depress—it can stifle hope, and, without hope, life cannot unfold.

True guilt is a deeper, more inner experience. It is a guilt that comes from a debt we incur to our own existence when we feel we have not been true to our self, living from out of our true nature.

When there is good reason for us to feel guilty, if, for instance, we intended to hurt someone, it is important that we forgive ourselves, for it is only out of self-forgiveness that a sense of remorse can move toward a longing to set things right with the other. Unrelenting guilt and self-punishment condemn us to an incapacitating sense of shame. The shame of guilt paralyzes us and prevents us from the opportunity to repair the hurts we have caused.

It helps if we can sort out our false guilt from our authentic guilt. When we can be with our true guilt in a spirit of self-forgiveness, our unrelenting guilt softens into regret. These softer feelings carry pain, for they contain true sorrow for our acts of omission and commission, and perhaps a sorrow for what may not be able to be repaired for the one to make repair with is no longer with us.

Unlike the hardening of guilt, regret and sorrow are feelings that can move through us, waves of hurting letting us know that we are real and human and feeling what is ours to be felt. In this way, our grief is soft and alive and honoring of our love and loss.

If you regret that you were less than who you wanted to be toward a loved one who is gone, be aware that you are like every other frail human being who has fallen short. You realize that you cannot repair the past, but you can find ways to bring your gestures of repair into the future. In this way, you are putting down seeds of new beginnings, of new hope and new life. This is the true medicine that releases the depression that is partner to the severe punishment of guilt.

The man who feels guilty that he could not love his mother can go on to show his love to others. The woman who cannot go back to re-make a failed marriage can manifest her desire for wholeness in other relationships. With guilt, life is strangled. Guilt softened into regret allows life to move again. The soft sorrow of regret deepens our awareness of how fragile and precious life is and how deep is our intention to care for the lives of others with the best of our selves.

## *Guided meditation: Softening guilt into regret*

*Set time aside in which to contemplate any guilt you might feel toward the one you are grieving.*

*Sense the strands of guilt you might feel and, with compassionate presence for your human frailty, hold an intention to let your guilt soften into the sadness of regret.*

*Close your eyes and allow yourself to sense someone approaching you from behind.*

*Sense this one approaching you to be a wise and compassionate being who is standing quietly behind you with their hands coming to rest gently upon your shoulders.*

*Sense that this person knows you in all your frailty, but still holds you with a spacious, accepting heart.*

*She understands how you try to be a full human being and how, when you fall short, you try and try again.*

*Do you know this person or is it a wise stranger who has come to support and guide you?*

*Ask this wise person for guidance, ask for help to move toward self-forgiveness.*

*If you wish, you may speak aloud to your wise companion. "Please help me, wise one, to soften my guilt. Please show me how. I want to be released into forgiveness."*

*Listen to what your wise companion says to you.*

*After hearing what your wise companion has spoken to you, sense this person turning to leave you.*

*Feel the imprint of their strong and tender hands still upon your shoulders.*

*Know that you can call upon this person at any time to come and place their hands of compassion upon your shoulders.*

*All you need do is close your eyes, come to your breathing, and call for the wise, compassionate one to come to you.*

*Be aware of how the wisdom of this wise one knows how*

*we are each here in this life to practice how to love—ourselves and others—to practice how to forgive ourselves and others.*

*And you well can hold yourself in the same way, with compassion for your human frailty and for your devotion to repair the ways in which you may intentionally or unintentionally caused hurt.*

*Know, too, that the one for whom you grieve also did her best.*

*Be aware if you carry blame toward her.*

*Breathe and allow these feelings to melt into regret for how each of you missed the mark, lost the opportunity to make things right with one another before the end.*

*Breathe out and, as you do so, free yourself from blame and free your loved one from guilt.*

*Ask yourself, what aspect of yourself fell short with your loved one?*

*What did you do or what did you not do then that you can do now?*

*What can you carry forth into your life with wholeness in order to repair the past as you move into your future?*

*What kindnesses can you give? What changes can you make?*

*How can you live better now, truer to your self, with others in your life who are dear to you?*

*See yourself living into the future in these ways.*

*Place this vision into your heart so it may go with you like a compass and a prayer.*

## In your journal

If you are sitting with the inner process of turning your guilt to regret, or if you are sitting with lifting blame from the one who is dying or has already passed, or if you are sitting with the longing of you true self wanting to speak what is in your heart. . .

Let yourself write a letter of forgiveness, perhaps to yourself, perhaps to the one in your life who is dying or has died. You may or may not give your letter to the one who is dying. The one who has already died will not read you words.

But you will have spoken your intention for letting go, letting be onto the page.

Your heart will hear your words of regret, of longing to live now from you true vulnerable being.

Those who live on with you will receive your letter without ever reading it. They will read it in the gestures of your softened heart.

And we do not know: The thin thread that joins the living and the departed may carry the vibration of your forgiveness to the one who is dying or already gone. Your letter may reach both the hidden places of your heart and the hidden places where the one you have written to abides.

# 23.

## *The soft heart of regret*

ONTHS AFTER ALEX'S WIFE DIED, *he wrote a letter to her in his journal: "Dear Natalie, We never unwound the hurts, the knots of anger, the disappointments, the pent-up needs. They got all mixed up with our love. I want you to know that during those last months we had together, I did unravel them. Not with words, but with my love.*

*As you grew weaker, I began to know how deeply I would miss you. I felt softer, gentler, and closer to you. I never found the words to unravel things. But please know, I did the best I could. I sense you felt how I was trying to communicate my deep love for you. I know my love meant a lot to you. I wish I had the words then that I have now; I wish I'd been able to tell you of my love and the healing it has brought me. I so regret that I could not unravel my hurt and anger that congealed over the years so that I could give you the healing words of my pure love."*

After the death of someone we love, very few of us—if we are truthful with ourselves—are left with the memory of a perfect relationship. We are human and perfection, except for moments in time, is not part of our nature. As the months and years go by after our loss, we are left to do the heart's work of meeting the inevitable pain of unrealized hopes in our relationship interrupted by death. We are left to resolve the anger, resentments, and disappointments that have survived our loss. The work of relationship goes on for us who are left here.

As we meet what was left unresolved in our relationship, as we unravel old knots, we come to understand in the depths of our being that it is love that survives when all else is lost. It is the strength of our love that fuels our devotion to heal what remains unhealed. On The Path of Grief, we learn that it is love that survives all else, opening us to a peace that awaits us in our sorrow.

Love is the bridge that moves us forward in our grief. For many of us, the path to that bridge is forgiveness, of our self, of our loved one. Forgiveness was what Alex needed in order to heal the unresolved and unspoken with his wife. He needed to forgive himself for not having softened toward her sooner and forgive her for dying before they could find words to bridge their differences. Love will lead us to forgiveness and forgiveness will lead us to love. In our hearts, they live side by side.

*As Alex continued to write to his wife in his journal, he continued to heal: "I regret we didn't have more time to share, to heal before you died. I will carry this regret in my heart as a reminder to face with love all the complex feelings that come, especially with our children."*

I hear a prayer in Alex as he faces his regret, a prayer to connect to the healing regret can bring to all of us.

### A Prayer to Soften the Hardened Heart

*May I lay a hand of tender mercy upon the hardening of my heart. May what has hardened into blame or anger or hurt turn toward the softness of regret.*

*May the soft sadness of my regret release me from the starvation that comes from closing off my love.*

*May I accept the imperfections of my human nature and the imperfections of those I love.*

*May my regrets live side by side with the power of Love.*

*May I be aware of the moments my heart hardens.*

*May I turn those moments toward kindness—*

*Kindness toward myself, toward my loved ones, and to all living, vulnerable, frail, mortal beings.*

*May my simple acts of kindness be for the memory of my loved one, who has been my teacher of turning my hard heart into a soft, loving heart of regret.*

## Guided meditation: The light of love waits to touch you

*During this week, sit in quiet meditation and ask yourself:*

*What feelings are blocking my love?*

*Do I feel anger, disappointment, judgment, hurt?*

*What do I need to forgive myself for? Forgive the other for?*

*Allow yourself to sit quietly, naming your feelings, each of them sensing where they sit in your body.*

*Try not to label your feelings as negative or positive, as good or bad.*

*Know how anger is not necessarily a negative feeling, nor is disappointment or any other feeling.*

*Just sense where your feelings sit in your body, breathe into them.*

*Let yourself understand that feelings are simply innocent bodily sensations.*

*Allow yourself to connect with feelings, turning to body sensations.*

*Know that the only thing negative is when your feelings block the flow of aliveness.*

*Feel and sense how this blockage stops sacred life moving through you.*

*Be kind to yourself, simply breathing, sensing.*

*Breathe, relax, go slow, take time to sense deep within, quietly naming your feelings as they arise.*

*Feel a warm light in the center of your heart.*

*Know it as the light of love shining forth from the great heart of the universe.*

*Focus your awareness on this light, on this sensation of warmth.*

*Is this light a candle flame? Is it a bright or soft light? Does it have a color?*

*What does the light of love in your heart feel and look like?*

*Sense and feel how your heart is holding light at its center.*

*Allow this light to find, touch, and melt whatever calls to be softened within you.*

*You may lift up to the light whatever is old, used up, no longer needed, whatever is ready to be released and melted into the compassionate light of your heart.*

*Sense and feel how as the light touches feelings not ready to soften—hurt, pride, anger, resentment, judgment—it lingers there with an enduring patience.*

*This light knows how hardened feelings take time to soften.*
*Be as patient with yourself, as the light of love is patiently with*

*you. Breathe and allow the softening, the melting to happen. Sense how this softness pulsates inside of your loving and stays open to the light.*

*Now, sit, be still, and place your hand over your heart.*

*Know how this light of love is always there, even when you cannot find it, even when you are lost in the darkness of hard, unmoving pain.*

*Know love always remains, always prevails, always heals, always waits for you.*

*Sit quietly. Hear your heart whispering to you:*

*"In the end, love is all that remains, all there is, all I need."*

*Whenever you wish to touch or be touched by the light of great love, simply place your hand upon your heart, come to quiet, and wait.*

*Breathe.*

*Allow love to come, ever so softly, to touch you and light to warm and soften your heart.*

## *In your journal*

Sit in the company of your open journal, pencils or crayons, and a lit candle.

Bring awareness to your heart. Without judgment, allow yourself to sense:

Is my heart soft, vulnerable, broken, covered over?

Do each of these layers live in my heart?

Take your time to see with your inner vision, with your deep sensing:

Does your heart have a crust over it for protection?

Perhaps you see your heart both soft, open, and vulnerable and hardened, each in turn.

Whatever appears, breathe, open yourself to accept what appears without judgment.

Draw and write what you see of your heart.

Let whatever is there speak on to the page.

And then allow the light of love to softly spread over what you have drawn and written.

Allow the energies of these forces to move into your heart.

As you are touched with the power of these energies, be aware of any softening your heart longs for in relation to your loved one who is dying or has already departed.

Write a letter from your heart to give words to your regrets and to your love.

Perhaps you will share this letter with your loved one.

Whether you do or not, know that the simple writing of both your regrets and your love will create transformation in your heart to be felt by all those close to you.

# 24.

# *I allow grief pain to move through me*

IMAGINE A FREE-FLOWING STREAM; see how easily and swiftly the water moves along its smooth banks. Now see a dammed-up stream. See how the stagnant water accumulates rocks and debris that block the natural movement of the stream.

You and I are like these streams. Our feelings are meant to move through us like ripples and waves, but too often they become dammed up, creating emotional and physical blockages. Watch how animals or children who feel safe express their emotions. Notice how their feelings spontaneously move through and out of their bodies; tears, rage, laughter, and happiness all ripple and flow through their soft, open bodies. Their muscles may tense with fear or anger, and then the tightening loosens into tears, screams, or laughter. Wave after wave of precious life streams through the wide-open emotional channels of their bodies.

As adults, something has happened along the way to stop the free flow of our emotions. We hold back, get blocked, and cut ourselves off from our feelings. We do this because we hear and attend to the messages from our families, our culture: Don't cry. Don't be afraid. Don't be needy. Don't be angry.

Be a big girl. Be a good girl. Be a big, brave boy. Don't bother anyone with your feelings.

These messages are heard in every part of our bodies—in our muscles, in our deep organs, in our heart and breathing—they wire our nervous system. So, it is no surprise that, in time, we become like the blocked stream, our feelings dammed, our intense and naked emotions—anger, love, loss, wanting, grief—become caught and held inside our bodies, muscles, organs, and breathing.

When we cut ourselves off from our feelings, we tighten with the sheer effort it takes to hold them back. We tighten against sorrow and pain, against the flow of tears. We use our energy to hold back the dam, fearing we will be flooded. To feel how strong this tension can be, take a moment and purposely contract the muscles in your arms, your hands, your legs, your stomach, mouth, and brow; hold them tight and tighter, as tight as you can. See and sense how rigid you become, how constricted. Feel the interplay of your feelings and emotions with your physical body—notice how your body and your feelings are one, this feeling, that tightening of sinew, muscle. As your feelings and your body harden, the stream of your life energy constricts and stops flowing.

*When my daughter died, I cried for months and months and then threw myself into work from morning 'til night. Work was demanding and, at the same time, what I thought of as lifesaving, requiring that I deny my tears the space and time they needed to flow freely. I carried my sunglasses wherever I went just in case tears broke through the dam. I believed that if I cried, I would crumble, be unable to work, be unable to go on liv-*

*ing. Sometimes the tears would break through. I would run to the bath-room to cry, "Pull myself together!" and return to the tasks of work.*

*Most of the time, my tears had to wait until after work. Even then, more often than not, I could not, would not, cry. Over time, as I re-fused to shed my tears, I developed severe sinus pain. Unbeknownst to me, tight, trapped tears were backed up in my sinuses, needing to be drained every month by a doctor.*

*One of my doctors gently suggested my sinus trouble might be the result of locked-up tears. His suggestion helped me to give my tears permission to flow. Every day, I made time to lay down on the carpet, at first to relax the tightness in my chest, then to slowly allow the re-lease of my tears. My tears flowed and flowed: They knew it was their time to allow the pain of sorrow to soften and move. Within a few weeks, I had no more sinus pain, no more trips to the doctor. I made time each day for the tears of longing for my daughter, for the tears of unbearable sorrow. As I cried and cried, allowing tears to move, I learned my tears would not drown me.*

*I realized I had been terrified to allow my tears because I thought if I allowed them the dam would break, the flood would go on forever, and I would be completely broken and unable to work or function at all. However, to the contrary, by lying down beside my heartbreak, by tenderly embracing the very feelings I had been protecting myself from, I found the solace I had longed for, found my way to balance time for unbearable sorrow and time for work. I learned the lifesaving differ-ence between being flooded and allowing grief feelings to flow. I would lay on the carpet, inviting my tears, listening to them as they flowed and slowly took on a rhythm that both held and sounded my sorrow. And then quiet would come and I would rest there, wrapped in solace.*

I share my experience of how I unblocked my tears and released physical symptoms, so you can see how one person came to understand the importance of being present to the tightening and feeling the tension caused by resistance to feel grief pain. I share my experience, not to tell you what to do, or how to do it, but to let you know there are many ways for you to connect to what is sealed away behind your blocked feelings. Don't think you must spend 20 minutes each day lying on the carpet, crying. That was my way. You will find your own time and way to release the tightening, the tension, the feelings, and the tears you are holding back and that hold you back.

## Guided meditation: Softening the tight place

*Set aside time to be with yourself in your place of solitude.*

*Plan not to respond to any interruptions: Don't answer the telephone or door-bell.*

*Sit in a comfortable chair or lie down. Loosen anything tight.*

*Begin to relax. Breathe down into your body.*

*Listen to your breathing. Be aware of the rising and falling and of the pause in between your breaths.*

*Perhaps you wish to listen to some quieting music.*

*Notice any tight places in your body*

*Let your chest and your back relax into the chair, floor, or bed.*

*Settle down. Feel the support you can lean into.*

*Begin to scan your body. Notice. Is your stomach tight?*

*If so, make it even tighter. Then ask it to relax and loosen, breathe into it.*

*Notice if your jaw is clenched. If so, tighten it more and then let it loose if it is ready to. Take your time. Breathe slowly in and out, resting in the pause between breaths.*

*Let each part of you know it is okay to relax and release. It is okay for tears to come.*

*Sense how you are letting go and letting your body simply be.*

*Take your time to find any other areas of tightness in your body.*

*As you continue to relax and find new areas of tightness, don't try to change it. Let it be.*

*Breathe. Be present with it. Place your hand on it.*

*Let yourself sense and feel: What is in this tightness? What is it holding? Breathe.*

*Ask the tightness: What are you tightening against? What don't you want to feel? Breathe.*

*Let the tightness under your hand answer you, tell you what it is holding back to protect you from feeling.*

*Maybe the tightness is holding back tears, loneliness, the ache of missing, anger, or despair.*

*Breathe in, breathe out. Maybe the tightness is protecting you from feeling the emptiness of your loss.*

*Breathe in, breathe out.*

*Let the feelings come, let them speak to you.*

*Let your feelings and your body sense tender touch of your hand.*

*Sense your breathing ease as you allow your difficult feelings.*

*Sense your acceptance and welcoming of whatever feelings arise.*

*You may feel a softening, or you may continue to feel a tightness that will not soften.*

*Know that this tightness is protecting you from feeling too deeply right now.*

*Let the tightness know it can ease, for you are ready for it to soften its protection.*

*If not, let it know it can be there.*

*Accept whatever is present. Breathe acceptance: Talk to*

*yourself, to your body:*

*"I accept whatever you feel body. I know feelings will come through this wall of tightness when it is time. Until then, know you are felt and known under my tender hands."*

*As you close this meditation, thank your body, your emotions, and the protection of your tightness for taking good care of you.*

## *In your journal*

As you practice this meditation, you may want to keep your journal beside you and write down the feelings that come.

You may see images or shapes of what is tightening or softening within you.

You may draw the tightness, how it may begin to flow or does not flow.

What images arise out of the tightness? What colors? What sounds? What sensations?

As you write, you may ask the area in your body that is closed, "What are you holding against? What do you need?"

Allow time for the voice of the tightness in your body to speak onto the page.

Allow the tightness to be, to have its time.

As you give it your hand and your listening, tightness will speak to you.

Let your tightness do the writing. Sense any softness as writing comes.

Listen to what is at its center. Let the center of tightness speak into its softening.

Write and draw what you see and hear at the center of tightness.

Write and draw the movement from tightening into softening.

Let it all speak onto the blank page.

# 25.

# *I allow my grief to move physically*

D OROTHY SAYS, "I DON'T KNOW WHAT'S WRONG WITH ME. *All I want to do is sleep. I can't think of doing anything else." She wonders if she is ill, but a medical examination shows nothing wrong. It is clear to her family and friends that since her husband's death six months earlier, Dorothy walks and talks and sits with a lethargy they have not seen in her before: She lacks the desire to participate in her everyday activities, and her family says she seems shell-shocked.*

During our grief, our intense feelings of sorrow, tears, anger, and regret may become so intense that they congeal and grow stagnant within our body. We become lifeless. This is what I call "grief depression." On The Path of Grief there is often a balance we come to between our feelings of sorrow that are flowing and our need to be quiet and still in the space of solace. We often lose our balance in the struggle between the torrent of our intense feelings and our need for healing solitude. Sometimes our solitude and stillness lose their openness to allow feelings to flow in balance with our need to be quiet and still. It is when stillness loses its openness that we are in danger of becoming depressed—held back, damped down, unable to move through the normal flow of our feelings.

Grief depression is grief that has stopped moving, grief that no longer flows like a stream, taking its natural course. And when we feel this shutting down of the natural movement of our grief—this depression of our feelings—our bodies reflect this stagnation. Our shoulders slump, our head droops, and our posture mirrors the shutdown of our life's energy flow.

If you are experiencing grief depression, you will benefit from doing something you probably *really* do not want to do: being more physically active. Even just a small increase in movement can help make possible a small opening for life to move. Notice if you don't want to move, don't want to get up, go out, or do anything. This inaction can be your wakeup call to get moving, to help lift yourself out of your grief depression.

You don't have to start big. Simply start small. Ask friends to take turns going on short, slow walks with you. Work slowly, easily in your garden. Take leisurely swims or stroll with your dog. Clean the house, just a little at a time. These activities require no mental effort. You don't have to think or plan.

Physical activity is rote, routine, pure movement. Your heart and mind don't have to participate. Just your body moving, one step at a time, from one place to the next, inch-by-inch, helping your body sense that there is still energy, there is still movement, there is still life—there is still the hope of moving on.

If depression is blocked life force, by physically moving, we begin to use the energy we have, and when we do, we create small openings for our life force to move through. As we become more active, more oxygen enters our lungs and blood stream and our entire body is nourished, making us feel more alive. Nothing rigorous is required. Modest physical activity is good medicine right now to help you heal the depression caused by your grief.

In your movement, you affirm your devotion to the movement of life's energies. You re-affirm your commitment to go on living. Somehow, you are making a promise to the one who is no longer alive that their life force will go on being breathed in yours.

*My friend Jim is grieving the loss of his wife. He asks me to take a walk with him. We head to the lovely reservoir in our neighborhood where Jim often went running. But today he can barely muster the energy to walk. So, we walk slowly, not talking much.*

*After a while, our conversation starts up. Nothing important: We notice a tree, a row boat on the lake, the clear sky. Small talk, nothing important. The important thing is:*

*We are moving and breathing in the green of life.*

*As we continue our walk, I sense Jim's energy slowly rising. His body is more upright. He moves and speaks with more vitality. His face has more color than I've seen in weeks. Jim even laughs at the squirrels chasing each other across our path.*

*He laughs, and then he is crying. I am relieved. Jim is coming back to life. I see the dark cloud of his depression lift a bit, a beginning, during our walk.*

*Jim is finding a way to slowly, gently keep his grief moving in his life. He is beginning to understand that when his body moves, it opens to everything inside and all around him and connects him to his feelings, his laughter, his tears, and to life moving all around him. He is beginning to see his grief as a stream rippling through his body, soul, and spirit, a stream he can allow to flow as he walks with a friend beside him.*

*Upon saying goo-bye, we agree that I will come at the same time tomorrow to walk again. We walk together several mornings a week for the next few months. Jim's depression lifts. He carries on. I know he will play our walks forward for, just like me, he knows how healing it is to move our stuck energies in the company of a caring other.*

## Guided meditation: Breath movement meditation

*Begin this meditation by sitting comfortably or lying down.*

*Let your body move in a soft and easy way until it is comfortable.*

*Allow your breath to come, breathing in and breathing out.*

*Feel yourself relaxing, notice the space between your breaths.*

*Notice your breath moving in you, allow it to slow, to become deep, and soft, and easy.*

*Begin to gently breathe in through your nose and out through your mouth.*

*As you breathe in, breathe in a healing light.*

*See the color of this healing light—white, silver, gold, blue.*

*Notice what healing color enters your body as you breathe in.*

*Sense yourself receiving the healing life energy of this color with every breath you take.*

*Sense the energy of this healing light, moving to every part of your body: through every organ, every cell, through the flowing river of your blood stream.*

*As you exhale, imagine you are breathing out an old gray smoke that carries away the old energies of your body, of your feelings, of your life.  Anything your spirit is ready to release.*

*See this old gray smoke rise out of you, float out your window, rise into the sky, and fade into the heavens.*

*Sense how the old gray smoke turns to the healing light.*

*See the color of the healing light as it comes to you.  Let it enter you.*

*As you inhale, breathe in the healing light coming to you from the heavens.*

*Let it move slowly through every one of your organs: your lungs, heart, liver, spleen, intestines, gall bladder, muscles, and bones.*

*See the healing light move through the flowing river of your blood stream.*

*Sense the healing light moving into every cell of your body.*

*Feel how the healing light knows your grief and is bringing healing to it as you breathe it.*

*Keep breathing out the old gray smoke and breathing in the healing light for as long as you wish.*

*Sense how this powerful, gentle breath movement meditation is releasing what is old and used up, bringing you renewed life energies, quieting your nervous system.*

*Now, if you wish, while sitting or standing, raise your arms slowly as you breathe in and lower them as you breathe out.*

*Allow your movements to be simple and slow, moving with your breath.*

*Allow your arms to rise up as you breathe in, reaching toward the hidden heart of the heavens.*

*Allow your arms to lower as you breathe out, reaching toward the hidden heart deep in the earth.*

*With your open hands, bring these energies as a blessing*

*into your heart.*

*Allow them to reach into any dark grief places anywhere in your body.*

*These simple movements will open the flow of energy in your body and prepare you for some small activity, perhaps taking a walk alone or with a friend. The company of a friend may help you leave the house and give you the physical, emotional, and spiritual support you need as you begin to nurture your life force.*

*As you walk, feel your feet on the ground, sense your breath moving through your body.*

*With every breath you take, say, "I am alive. Even if I am sad, even as I grieve, I am alive, and this makes my loved one smile for me."*

## *In your journal*

After doing your breath movement meditation or after taking a walk alone or with a friend, come to sit in your quiet place.

Perhaps with a glass of water beside you.

While you sit, feel the movement of life's energies in your body.

Sit and listen to any words, feelings, or sounds these energies hold.

You may wish to write about them.

Let the life energies speak upon the page.

Or simply draw the color and movement of the energies alive in you just now.

Remember, these energies that have opened in your movement do not have to be happy or even life-affirming; they can be sad and dark. They can be just as they are.

What matters is that there is a vibration of life, your living.

# 26.

## *I find solace in solitude*

WHEN A PERSON HAS LIVED to an old age and comes to the completion of a well-lived life, that person's survivors may well know a deep peace and gratitude for having journeyed to the end of a loved one's path in this life. When our loss is unexpected or untimely, our grief journey will be different. Each of us will have to create our own map and our own timetable. Although each of us must move through grief in our own way, there may be familiar steps along the way shared with others who have travelled the same path. We may experience the shock of death's finality, even if it has been coming for a long time.

After death, we may live through long, empty nights. We may feel lost. We may feel numb, bewildered, unmoored from familiar ground.

We may find ourselves searching for our loved one as we are out walking. Sometimes, for a moment, we think we see our loved one— on a sidewalk, in a crowd, turning a corner. For a moment, we may sense our loved one coming to us, in the fluttering of a butterfly or the flight of a bird, in a song or in our dreams. The veil between our loved one in death and ourselves in life is sometimes thin and other times is utterly impenetrable. We all know the pain of struggling to reconcile ourselves to the finality of our loss. We all know the struggle of going on while feeling we cannot go on.

In your grief, you may feel cut off from life, thrown into the utter aloneness that permeates your days and nights. You have come to a place called loss," to a desert without any sign post—thrown into a vast open space between all that was and not yet knowing what, if anything, will come of new life, you join the tribe called the in-between people.

If you abide in this in-between space of loss, if you accept the desert journey through grief, your aloneness may slowly be touched by the manna—the blessing—of solitude. You may feel something come to touch you in the depths of your being, a sense of quiet, a quiet that holds all that is, a sacred quiet, a quiet of compassion.

*Sandra talks about living alone after the death of her husband: "At first it was excruciating. As I moved through the long nights alone, sat alone by the lake looking up at the empty sky and walked aimlessly through the parks and city streets by myself, I experienced a depth of aloneness I had never known before. At first, the pain I felt was the pain of having been suddenly ripped apart from my husband by death, a ripping off my chest." Sandra places her hand on her chest, recalling the pain of fresh grief.*

*"As I live with this pain, I find myself more and more able to take comfort the silent moments. For a time, a sense of emptiness and depression washed over me. The silence was an aching, empty, bottomless silence. Then, as I slowly grew more used to the silence, silence went on just being silence, and I felt something within it touch me with an unexpected sense of peace, like a vessel holding my aloneness and my pain."*

*In this ground of solitude, Sandra felt her beloved husband's presence as she recalled precious moments they shared. She became aware of a tender smile upon her face.*

*Out of the empty silence of grief, we slowly come to find the solace of solitude. At first, we are only aware of fleeting moments of respite from our unrelenting grief, but eventually we may notice for the first time that, beside the physical ache of our grief, we sense an oasis of healing quietness. As we sit and as we walk with our solitude, we discover how it touches us with the soft hand of compassion. We find a capacity to be alone that we never knew before because somehow, we come to sense that we are alone and yet not alone, our solitude a part of the solitude at the center of all things.*

Like Sandra, may you come to find yourself aware once again of precious moments of life: sunlight warming your dulled body, seeing with wonder a child taking its first steps, stopping to watch the movement of a leaf in the breeze. May you come to see the ordinary happenings of life with a sense of revelation, as if for the first time. May you discover the manna in the barren desert of your soul, the nourishing awareness of life that pulses through your grief.

May you feel the nearness of your loved one, woven into the moment when you stand still beside the deep solitude at the center of a wild flower that you stop to behold at the side of the road. May you slowly discover how, in the dry, stark desert of your grief, there comes a most tender sense of solitude, touched as never before by the sacred aliveness at the center of the smallest things of life.

## Guided meditation: Coming to a place of solitude

*Sit quietly in a comfortable place. Listen to the silence.*
*Close your eyes.*
*As you become quiet, feel your breath.*
*As you breathe in through your nose, sense how you receive*

*life.*

*As you breathe out through your mouth, sense how you give to life.*

*Let your breath guide you to a quiet space within your body.*

*Put your hand on this place, perhaps on your heart, or your solar plexus, or your stomach.*

*Find the quiet place and keep your hand gently there as you continue to breathe.*

*Sense your hand and your breath rising and falling as you breathe.*

*You do not have to make any effort at all. Feel yourself being breathed.*

*See yourself breathing in a beautiful, clear, radiant light.*

*See the color of this light.*

*Let it fill the quiet place below your hand into your body.*

*See the space become larger until it becomes a peaceful place in nature.*

*See yourself there.*

*Look around. Are you near a lake, on a mountaintop, in a garden, by the sea, in a chapel?*

*Wherever you find yourself, know this as your special place of solace and solitude.*

*Be here. Be still. Breathe quietly. Breathe the peace of solitude.*

*Sense the silence within you and all around you.*

*Does the silence have a vibration? A color? Take your time to sense the quality of the silence in your place of solitude.*

*Welcome any sadness, any tears, any sad or joyful song of your love and loss.*

*Let it all be held in the sacred silence and solace that surrounds you inside and out.*

*Know how this place of solitude is always here for you.*

*All you need do is come to your breath and place a hand gently on your body.*

*Your special place of silence is always right there, just under your breath and your hand.*

*You can always enter this place where the peace of solitude awaits you.*

## *In your journal*

Take your time; bring your awareness to your breathing.

In your journal, write of what your place of silence in nature is like for you.

Write in detail as you would in calling a dream back to you.

In your journal, reenter your waking dream and write it as a story.

Write of all you see, hear, feel, and sense.

As you write, breathe in rhythm with this place of your solitude. Be there.

See where you sit, stand, or lie down in this place that is yours.

What waits to speak out of the silence from the depth of solitude?

Take your time, breathe, listen until you hear.

Perhaps there are words. Perhaps not sentences, just words that sound arise out of silence.

Perhaps there are no words, only sounds or subtle vibrations.

Wait and see, sense and feel, receive what comes.

Place them into our body and onto the page with your pen or colored pencils.

# 27.

## *Little things may trigger my grief unexpectedly*

SEVERAL MONTHS AFTER SALLY'S HUSBAND *Fred died, she was walking along the street with a friend on a lovely spring afternoon. It is one of those moments in which, without realizing it, she is not thinking about Fred. Then, her husband's barber passes and says a warm hello. Sally's tears and the wound of her grief open wide.*

When we lose someone, there are echoes of that person all around us—at home, in the local stores, out at dinner. You never know when you will be surprised by your grief.

*Some time after Ken lost his wife, he accepted an invitation from a friend to go to the movies. Sitting in the theater, he saw a man put his arm around the woman beside him. The ache of loss pierced Ken's heart, and he cried during the film. His friend reached over and touched his shoulder.*

There is no hiding from your grief. If it is fresh, you may well ache with the pain of an open wound.

Your friends and family members may try to help you close the opening. You may try yourself to close it, tightening your muscles, holding back the tears, choking down your words, holding in your feelings, afraid that if you stay open to the pain you will not be able to go on. Tightening against the opening of grief stores your feelings in places in your body where you tighten against the pain. Grief waits there, sometimes for many years, sometimes for a lifetime, sometimes into the life of your children who carry your unlived grief. Grief will wait forever for the opportunity to open and release.

When you are surprised by something that opens your grief, even long after you thought the opening had closed, be aware of attempting to tighten the muscles in your body, as if you are saying, "Pull yourself together, hold yourself up." Becoming aware of tightening, allow it to be and then slowly shift

to your breathing, breathing slowly and gently to the tight places, allowing them to soften, allowing your feelings to open. If tears want to come, let them. If you are with someone at dinner, in a store, or in the car, reassure that person that you are "just crying, it's all right." People who think they need to reassure you may need to be reassured by you. Let the people around you know this is something you need to do and can do. Let yourself know this.

If you do cry, if you do allow the feelings and the waves of your grief to move through you, you can sense them as ocean waves, waves moving in and out, in and out. See how the waves may roil and then become calm. This is how the waves of grief are, how our feelings of grief flow through us. To allow this free flowing of feeling is the only way to live with grief, letting the waves move as they will, breathing with them, riding the waves until they move out. Waves of feeling moving in, moving out.

It is not easy to stay open when your grief appears unexpectedly, like an uninvited guest. It helps if you have a friend like Ken's who can touch your shoulder and say, "Don't worry, it's okay, just cry, just let it go through you. There's no need to talk right now. I'm right next to you." In time, you find that you can befriend your own self when the grief waves come. You can be your own very good and wise friend. You can speak your friend's words to yourself, "Don't worry, it's okay, just cry, just let the waves go through, I'm here, beside you." Who is this friend speaking from within you? It is the one who, on your journey through grief, has grown a wise and tender compassionate heart, who can be there for you and for others as the waves wash over.

If you find yourself tightening because you have a knowing sense that you cannot carry the feelings for your loss because they are coming up at too many unexpected times in ways that are too often or too much, your wise self may take this as a signal to reach out for the help of a counselor or bereavement group.

### Guided meditation: I breathe with the waves of my grief

Coming to your quiet place at the end of your day, settle into your breathing, into your body.

As you breathe, let your awareness drift back over your day.

Allow yourself to call up any event that may have surprised you and opened your grief when you least expected it.

Allow this event to replay itself, perhaps finding yourself back there feeling the feelings you may have choked back earlier in the day.

Sense how your feelings are waiting for you to come to

*them, for you to be present for them, so they may have their life.*

*Take time now to offer any waves of grief the time and space to surface into your body awareness.*

*Let your awareness be gentle.*

*As you breathe, imagine yourself at the ocean.*

*Be there lying down at the shoreline, where the beach and the ocean meet.*

*Sense the rhythm of the vast ocean waves moving in, moving out, in, out.*

*Breathe in and out with the movement and rhythm of the ocean's waves.*

*Now allow your innocent feeling body to open to the waves, feel them moving into and through you.*

*Sense the waves coming in, washing your cells, your organs, your muscles, your breathing, your face, your eyes, your heart, washing through your grief body, your grief feelings.*

*Tenderly allow your grief to be washed over by the ocean waves.*

*Sense the ocean tides taking anything you are ready to release into the waves.*

*Sense them being carried by the waves out to the deepest part of the ocean and left there.*

*Let yourself feel how what you have released is at rest in the deepest part of the ocean.*

*After a while, let yourself sense the ocean becoming quiet.*

*Be there on the beach, resting on the line between the shore and the ocean.*

*Feel how the tide has gone out, how the ocean waters are quiet now.*

*Know how you are like the ocean, waves moving in and*

*out, in and out, and then the waves move out to sea, and everything is still.*

*Feel yourself as still as the ocean and the heavens, breathe stillness.*

*Be aware of a vast blue sky and golden sun above you.*

*Breathe in the clear blue of the heavens and the soft gold of the sun.*

*Let them fill you with pure, healing energy.*

*Sense and feel stillness all around you and deep within you.*

*Sense the quiet ocean and your quiet heart becoming quiet mirrors reflecting the vast blue sky.*

*Be there as long as you need to be.*

*In this space, you have all the time in the world.*

*Be there, with the natural rhythms of the tides,*

*with the natural rhythms of your grief.*

## *In your journal*

You know how in a fairy tale, everyone and everything can talk? An animal, a tree, a wolf, a bear.

In your journal, write as if the ocean came to talk to you.

Feel yourself as the ocean. Become the ocean.

Let the ocean tell you all about itself, its waves, its tides, its depths and rhythms, its movements.

Let yourself be surprised by what the ocean may tell you about itself.

Let the ocean tell you the ways in which it can be there for your grief. Write.

As you write, let yourself sense and feel the ways in which you are like the ocean, there for your grief.

# 28.

## *It is also myself I mourn*

WHEN SOMEONE CLOSE TO US DIES, we grieve for our loved one *and* we grieve for ourselves: We grieve *their* death and we grieve *our* loss. When we lose someone we love, we not only lose that one, we also lose the sense of self we knew *with them*. If we are no longer wife, husband, father, mother, friend, lover, daughter, son—if that role is fading away or gone—our sense of who we are in this life can become lost in the abyss of that unalterable absence.

This struggle with the loss of our relationship and our loss of identity becomes even more difficult when we realize we are also struggling with what remains, what is left behind despite the physical absence of the one we love: The physical relationship is over, for our loved one is gone, but our feelings, our days, our hours are still full of what remains. Even in their absence, we are still connected to those gone to death. Despite their physical departure, they are still with us, still connected to us by our ongoing love and commitment, still connected to us because of all the joys and trials shared, still connected through invisible cords of attachment that go on pulsating body to body. Even after they have been cut by death, the cords of loving connection may go on quivering with aliveness. The one we love is both lost to us and alive in us.

*Anna, a young wife of 24, lost her husband Bob in the Iraq war. Two days before he was due to return home, Bob and his buddy stepped on a landmine and were killed instantly. When I met Anna some time later, she told me she would always wear her wedding band, would always remain Bob's wife. She spoke of how her body still throbbed with desire for her husband, who had been dead more than a year. At the same time, she spoke of no longer feeling like Bob's wife; she felt that relationship had been amputated with his death and now felt like a phantom limb, a marriage, a husband, there and not there at the same time.*

Anna's experience reflects what many of us feel. While part of our identity in relationship with the one who has died will endure forever, another part of us feels stripped of that identity, caught in between two impossible feelings. This is a paradox we live with in grief. Anna told me she wanted to remarry, find a good father for her son. When she does remarry, after such a traumatic loss, she may slip and call her new husband "Bob" or murmur his name in her sleep. Hopefully, her new partner will understand how those we love and lose go on living within us, in our hearts, in our bodies, and in our memories, and so it is natural that our significant other will go on being a part of us—at times called out to from sleep in the middle of the night, sometimes honored with a marriage band that remains on our finger until it is, perhaps, one day ready to be removed.

What becomes most difficult to live with is our incapacity or refusal to grieve the loss of the world of our old identity. If we hold too tight to the memories, and stories, and history of our old relationship; if we continue to live life the way we used to live it; if we keep the house the same, thinking this will keep our loved one alive within us; if, in our effort to keep everything the same, we stop growing forward into Life; we are in danger of living a dead life, frozen in the past.

The dying of our loved one cracks us open, and the pain and shock make us want to recoil from the new, holding on to the life we knew. But if we find a way to stay open, if we live through the dying and the loss, in the broken spaces of our heart, new life can begin to emerge. You may not know who you are for a long while as you grieve the loss of your loved one and the loss of who you knew yourself to be.

As you wander the landscape of loss, you may have no sense that hidden seeds of new being, seeds of a new way *to be,* are growing deep in the dark crevices of your grief. Perhaps all you can feel now is cold, aching darkness. In your grief, you are not yet able to sense the possibilities of new life contained in these seeds, for seeds take their own time to grow. As seeds of new hope and new life incubate in the barren terrain of your grief, they somehow need the darkness of your grieving for the mystery of new beginnings to open. Darkness and time.

Waiting for a new sense of self to arrive *is* like waiting for a train: We read the newspaper, have a conversation with the person sitting next to us, stare into space, write in our journal, hope the train isn't delayed, hope it never comes, fearing what lies ahead or that nothing lies ahead. You may find yourself in prayer, whatever that may mean to you, perhaps for the first time, praying for something or someone to come and touch you with aliveness while you wait to find your way.

When you are forced by grief to leave the life you have known, leave the *self* you have been, you face one of life's biggest challenges. You think you are lost for good. But in time, somehow, out of somewhere, there arise glimmers of a new self. Perhaps Anna will go on wearing her old wedding band in devoted connection to her dead husband. Perhaps, too, as she allows the grief over the end of *herself as "wife"* to release, as she opens to something new to come forth for her, perhaps then the blessing of one day wearing another wedding band will be hers. Perhaps in her new life, Anna will sense the aliveness of her abiding connection with Bob across the thin veil between life and death.

The new self that arises from the ashes of your grief is actually not so new but is the embodiment of the essential qualities that make you who you are, now forged in the fire of your grief and guiding you to live your true nature. In the tender movement of time and healing, it is our core nature, now woven with strands of the core of the one departed, that comes like a devoted old friend to carry and guide our life forward.

## *Guided meditation: Seeds of new life*

*Listen to and honor the part of you that cannot bear to say goodbye to your relationship.*

*Listen to any loss of identity you are feeling that asks to be grieved.*

*Perhaps you cannot bear to feel your loss of the self you were and still long to be.*

*Perhaps you cannot bear feeling the emptiness of suffering, the loss of your own self.*

*Perhaps you feel you too have died, feel like a ghost of your former self.*

*Let your feelings be, listen, breathe.*

*Listen, alongside the "you" that mourns a loss of your self as you have known it, do you sense any small whispers of new beginnings stirring within you?*

*Know these stirring as the beginnings of your unfolding into new life.*

*As you sense these stirrings, let yourself be aware that your loved one is moving on and wants for you to do the same. Sense how your loved one wants you to have your aliveness and, in doing so, carry on his or her essential being.*

*Listen: Hear your loved one whisper to you what she or he wants you to carry of your relationship as you move into life.*

*Let yourself know how the essence of what lived between you will live on in your new beginning.*

*Sense what is stirring and opening up in your life.*

*Ask what nourishment it needs from you.*

*Just as newborns need their every need met, this new dawning in you needs tending.*

*Breathe light and oxygen to this fragile new life opening in you.*

*Recognize and acknowledge the sacred connection you are honoring as you hold fast to your old self.*

*Give this holding your gentle awareness and acceptance.*

*Know how you are releasing, letting go slowly, very slowly.*

*Respect how you need time and space to breathe into the letting go and how you need time to welcome small stirrings of new life to touch you.*

*As you go through your day, be aware how this newly emerging part of you wants to reveal itself to family and friends.*

*Listen and watch how can you express these emerging, delicate feelings of new life into the small, precious moments of your day.*

*Perhaps there is sadness also calling for your presence.*

*Side by side: gratitude for new life and sadness for the old and lost, each moving through you.*

*Waves of awareness—sadness and new life—moving through you with each breath.*

*Each wave calling for your presence, calling you to tend to each wave of feeling alive.*

## *In your journal*

Take the time to meditate on these questions:

What part of me is dying? has already died with the death of my loved one?

What part of me calls to slowly be released?

What part of me no longer has a place in my life?

Listen and meditate on these and any other questions asking for your presence.

Write your reflections upon these questions in your journal, take your time.

You may find yourself carrying the questions into your day and returning to write again in your journal in the quiet of the evening.

Listen closely to the part of you not ready to leave your old life, not ready to move on.

On one side of your journal, allow your tears, your anger, your heartbreak, your fear, your longing, your emptiness. Let yourself write all that you need to say about holding on to your known world.

On a facing page, write of any stirrings of seeds of new life you may sense.

These can be small stirrings, whispers, but they matter for they are bringing life.

Perhaps you will write: I went to buy some flowers today; I sat with someone at the coffee shop and felt like chatting, only for a few minutes, but that has been more than I could imagine over the past months.

Write of any small stirrings of life arising and of how you shall water them with your intention to be for life, for your sake and for your loved one, who whispers into your ear the blessing to go on. Listen and write.

# 29.

## *Living in the bardo spaces*

THERE IS A BUDDHIST UNDERSTANDING that, when someone dies, they enter a dark space with neither light nor signpost to show the way. This in-between space is called a *bardo*, leaving one life and not yet entering another. If the soul can abide the fear and trembling, the hope and despair, the unknowing of this space, light somehow comes to show a way. We, the living, also enter a bardo, an in-between space, the wilderness spaces between the old being falling away and the new being not yet glimpsed or glimpsed and filling us with both promise and dread of moving ahead.

Even if we throw ourselves back into the usual round of our life, in the core of our loss we are filled with the emptiness of not knowing where we are going. If we abide with awareness in the bardo state our grief brings us to, just as for the soul of the dead, we, too, are brought some dots of light to kindle our way.

These small bits of light usually come in totally unexpected moments, come as a surprise. They come beyond any rational thinking and often bring a keen sense of wholeness.

*Susan's husband died of lymphoma three years ago. After a month, she resumed her responsible position as an immigration attorney. Her days were busy, full, and rewarding to her. After her day's work, in the quiet, Susan became aware of how bereft she was, lost and not knowing what might bring meaning to help her go.*

*One night, Susan had a dream. She stood on the bottom of a staircase. She could not see where the staircase led. She could only sense the presence of her husband's spirit behind her, his gentle hand pressing her back to continue climbing the stairs. When she came to the top, Susan saw a doorway made of the most tender blue velvet, as blue as a clear blue sky.*

*While her husband was gone, Susan could feel the touch of his hand lingering on her back. Somehow, Susan knew that the deepest part of her would remain facing the door of blue velvet and that, when it opened, it would somehow reveal her way to her.*

Susan was surprised by a sense of wholeness and meaning brought to her by the dream. This is what often happens for us as we abide in the bardo, in the spaces in-between. Something wordless comes to surprise us from a hidden space, bringing a sense of possibility, of opening, of something being planted within us, something waiting to guide us that we may not yet fully see but have a felt sense, a glimmer of.

May you stay open. May you abide in the in-between spaces. May you be surprised by new life when it comes to touch you and guide your way.

## Guided meditation: Receiving a seed of new life

*Sit or lay down comfortably in your space of solace.*
*Allow your awareness to move through your bod.*
*Allow neck, shoulders, jaw, tongue, chest, stomach, arms,*

*legs, hands, fingers, feet, toes, every part of you, to relax.*

*Come to your breathing, in and out, in and out.*

*Be aware of the space between breathing in and out.*

*Know how built into your very breathing is the in-between space between one breath and the next.*

*Sense how you do not know when the next breath will come... or if it will come... and then the next breath comes.*

*As the next exhalation comes, allow it to become long, let it become a path.*

*See yourself on this path sense all around you.*

*What do you see? Hear? Sense? Feel?*

*Know that this path is leading you through a gentle forest until you find yourself standing in a meadow.*

*Be aware of the sky, of the air, of any sounds.*

*As you stand there in the beauty of your meadow, notice that from the far side, from out of the forest, there is a woman coming toward you.*

*Notice that she is an elder with white hair.*

*See that she is coming toward you, dancing her way.*

*See that, although she is crippled, she is still dancing.*

*Now, be aware of her in front of you.*

*See her lift her finger to her lips, signaling for you to become silent.*

*Notice that she is holding something very small in her other hand.*

*Now she is signaling you to open your mouth.*

*When you open your mouth, see that she places the smallest seed under your tongue.*

*Then she turns from you and silently, gracefully dances her way back across the meadow until she disappears into the forest.*

*Remain still, feel and sense this seed dropping and implant-*
*ing itself deep into you.*

*Know that you will carry the seed within you along the path*
*of your grief.*

*Know that in some way, beyond your understanding, the*
*seed will slowly open and grow, bringing healing and new being*
*to your life.*

*Feel your gratefulness to the old woman who came from*
*and returns to the mystery that brings us life.*

*Know how you are like this woman, crippled by the sorrow*
*of your grief and still open to receive the seed of new life.*

*Know how one day you shall give the seed to others as the*
*old woman gives the seed of life to you.*

## *In your journal*

Take the time to sit with each of the questions below.

With each question, be aware of what arises in your body, in your breathing.

You may wish to close your eyes or gently lower them.

Sense, and feel, and know all that opens for you. Take your time and write.

What is it like for you to live in the spaces of the bardo? To move through the forest? To come into the open space of the meadow?

What is it like for you to be met by the dancing, crippled woman in the meadow?

What does she look like? Is she familiar to you? Do you know her?

What is your sense of her? Who is she?

Take your time and write.

Why does she come to find you?

What happens for you when she instructs you to be silent?

And when she places the seed into your mouth?

Take your time. Write all that comes to you.

Draw what wants to be given shape and color upon your page.

# 30.

# *In grief, I discover tenderness*

I N THE WEEKS BEFORE SUSAN'S HUSBAND DIED, *he would sometimes turn to her and ask, "Will you be all right? Will you be okay when I die?" He is getting weaker by the day and knows he is dying. But Ellen cannot tell him she will be okay. She feels it would be a lie. She honestly doesn't know if she can or even wants to survive without him.*

*She can only say, "I don't know, but please, don't worry about me." But he does worry about her. As if to spare her, he chooses to die in the presence of their son, while Ellen is away. His last words are, "Help Mom pull through."*

*Her son and his family offer the consolation of their love and presence after her husband's death, but Susan can accept none of it. She does not turn her family away.*

*She is never unkind. She is just not present in spirit. Her family and friends are concerned she is becoming deeply depressed and they urge her to see a psychotherapist who deals with grief. That is how Ellen and*

*I met. During our first visit, we sat together quietly. Susan sensed it was okay to sit together in silence. She had no words, only her emptiness and the shock of still being alive while her husband was dead.*

*We sat in an atmosphere of stillness for several months. I was Susan's witness as she cried bewildered tears, sat in silence, talked a little, and returned to silence. Our shared silence allowed Ellen to know she could be alone because she was not alone, to know that it was safe to sit with her loss, with her mute loneliness. Neither of us pushed it away. She leaned into grief, and cried, and returned again to silence. There was comfort for Ellen as she stayed open to her grief. Some days, she brought a photo or two of her and husband, or a letter he had written to her, wanting me to see them and know about the life they had shared. The space between us became a shelter of solace we sat in together.*

*Both of us knew grief was not something to get over. Grief is not like an illness. Grief needs to be lived through. If we stay with our true feelings, lean into and allow even the feelings of no feeling, we open to the movement of feeling, which allows something more to move through us. When we stay open in our grief, something arises out of a mysterious, creative emptiness. What comes to us is a deepening sense of acceptance to be with what is and a letting go of what we believe our grief journey should be like.*

*On some days, Susan and I sat together while she lamented that she felt no feeling, just deadened, muted, gray, without life. All of this we named and witnessed without trying to change any of it. In some mysterious, inexplicable way, as Susan sat with whatever opened in her grief, and as I sat with her as witness, something in her turned. Out of the muteness, tears would appear and fall down her face, like water appearing in the desert.*

*Susan survived the loss of her beloved husband. She survived with a tenderness toward her own frailty, toward her weaknesses, toward the part of her that felt broken. She spoke of how she was surprised to find herself less angry, less irritable, less judging. She told me how, on the train, an older man with a cane had been offered a seat by several people. She had wept to see how kind and caring people were towards one another. Ellen said that, in the past, before her husband's death, she would never have taken note of such a small gesture of kindness. Today, she sees such gestures as acts of mercy we vulnerable, mortal humans give to one another.*

*Over the time we sat together, I was able to see a slight, gentle, sad smile line appear on her face, a line I sensed had never been there before, revealing someone deeply touched by life.*

*After several months together, Susan went away on a trip to New England by herself.*

*She wrote to me: "It's very quiet here. The bird sounds are quiet. The trees sway this way and that. The breeze moves through the trees. The poppies are gleaming. The sun streams down like sweet honey. My heart is full with a tender love for all that surrounds me, a shining, poignant wonder."*

*Susan finds words for her tender sense of the sacredness of life that has poured itself into her grief. This solace of tenderness cannot be made to happen. It cannot be forced in any way. It can only begin to shape us out of our aloneness, our silence, our willingness to stay open and bow to the ineffable seed of light that shines out of the darkness.*

## *Guided meditation: The tender touch of the hand-heart*

*As you sit quietly, be open to your tenderness toward yourself.*

*Sense where tenderness sits in your body, in your heart, in your breathing.*

*Know how tenderness can come to touch your grief.*

*If you cannot find tender heartedness within yourself, allow one of your hands to place itself on the other.*

*Now, with closed eyes, feel the hand touching you.*

*Imagine someone close to you come to place a hand of tender comfort upon you.*

*Let your tears, your anger, your sorrow, all that you are right now, be touched by this tender hand.*

*Sense the hand come to touch you knowing how precious your life is, how precious all of life is.*

*Let the hand touching you now become your own hand, reaching to yourself from your heart.*

*Breathe from your tender heart toward yourself and to all that is, toward everything and everyone.*

*Toward all that is precious and passing in this life, all that is asking to feel the touch of a compassionate hand.*

*If you wish, light a candle.*

*Sit with relaxed eyes as you watch the candlelight.*

*Sense how this soft candlelight is like the light at the center of your being, always there, present even if you cannot see or feel it.*

*Sense and know how this light at your center is the tender light of compassion.*

*Be aware of how this spark of light is always somewhere inside your darkness, waiting to shine forth.*

*Even if the light shines only for moments now, trust how one day you will see light all around you.*

*Know this light is also the light of the one you have lost, whose light has become part of the beauty of all life.*

*Feel and sense how this light of compassion within your heart moves to your hand.*

*Let your hand of tenderness touch your own heart and know how, on your grief journey, your hand/heart is coming to know how much it means to touch someone, who is grieving; to touch your own self; to touch those near and far; to reach the light of your heart; to where in the world there are souls in need of tender compassion.*

## *In your journal*

Sit in the silence in your place of solitude.

Light your candle.

As you sit and breathe, look into the light.

Feel the light of tender compassion in your heart's center.

Draw that light in your journal, draw slowly, with your breathing.

Feel the movement of the light, of the candle, and the light of your heart.

Allow this movement to reach your hand.

Allow the movement of your hand to write.

Allow the light of your heart to speak to your self, to any other, to any place wherefore the light of compassion is being called.

Take your time.

The light and the movement of your heart may be slow to speak.

Write and pause when you need to.

Sit with the light of the candle, with the light of your heart.

Write from that light, let it shine forth from your hand onto the page.

# 31.

## *My dreams show me the way*

OUR DREAMS CARRY MESSAGES we may not otherwise receive. They bring us to parts of ourselves that are deeper than our waking minds and offer us wisdom we may not otherwise uncover. Our dreams come to guide our waking selves, taking us below the tip of the iceberg of our daylight awareness.

*For some years after my daughter died, I dreamt that Leslie was waiting for me to come home to her at our old apartment. In my dream, I would climb the stairs, open the door, and there she would be. She was there for a moment and then everything suddenly evaporated, was gone, leaving me bereft once again.*

*One night, I dreamt the same dream, only different: I was coming home to the old apartment where Leslie was waiting for me. Only this time, she said, "Mommy, you don't need to come here anymore. I don't live here anymore. I live very far away where you can't come. Go home, Mommy, to where you live now. Mommy, I am where I live. Remember, Mommy, what I told you: "It is always light here; the sun always shines. And mommy, you can't come here."*

Thus, it was that from the deep knowing place of dream time that I was guided by my child to release myself from returning over and over again to our old home, released from trying to retrieve the old life we shared there. It was time for me to stop returning over and over again to the place of traumatic loss.

In dream time, where the veil between waking and sleeping drops away, loved ones who have died can speak to us and help us, as my daughter helped me. In my dream, she spoke to me and, with her help, I received the peace of completion. I never returned in dreams to searching for her in that old place again.

We may dream for years before we are able to accept the stark reality of our loss. Dreams from our deep, wise unconscious may come to help us heal years and years after our loved one has died. In the unconscious, our relationships remain forever. In our dreams, clock time has no place. In our dreams, we continue to work through our relationships and our losses. Dreams are to us what play is to children:

Children play the same game over and over and over again until they make sense of what is difficult for them to fully comprehend. "Dream time" helped release me from the vortex of traumatic loss.

Sometimes, especially when the death of our loved one has been traumatic, we are visited by nightmares. These *trauma dreams* often bring the same nightmare over and over again without a shift or change in the dream, a change that will turn us toward healing. When these *trauma dreams* persist without change over time, it is wise to find a trauma specialist in your area who works with dreams and can help you re-enter your dream and move it toward healing.

*Melanie's son, Karl, was critically wounded in a car crash. Rushed to the hospital, Karl was placed on life support. After two weeks, the doctor told Melanie and her husband, Ben, that Karl would spend the rest of his life comatose. Melanie wanted to release Karl from suffering. Her husband and the doctor supported her choice. She and Ben sat at Karl's bedside while his life support was removed and stayed with him for hours after his death. Although they both felt they had made the most loving decision they could make for their son, grieving was not simple.*

*Soon after Karl died, Melanie began to have nightmares in which she was killing her son. Her guilt and depression rooted deeper and deeper within her as her trauma dreams played night after night.*

*She and I entered dream time and faced the spirit of her son. She saw Karl's spirit surrounded by a golden light, at peace and beyond all pain. She saw her son in his unharmed body smiling down and expressing thanks to his mother for having the courage and love to release him.*

*Melanie wept as she spoke to the spirit of her son, "I will always love you. I will plant a beautiful Japanese maple tree in our garden where we can come to sit, me in body, and you, my beloved son, in spirit."*

In the waking dream, there is no separation between what happens in the place of *dream time* and what happens on the physical levels of our existence. There is a part of the right side of our brain called the limbic brain. This part of our brain carries the wisdom of knowing when things are brought to completion and can rest in a sense of wholeness. When Melanie opened her eyes, I could see on her face the quiet light of wholeness, healing and holiness. Her nightmares became fewer and farther between and then faded altogether. She planted the maple tree and found solace in simply sitting there, surrounded by the golden light of her son.

In my own healing and in my healing work with others, I have come to trust how *dream time* opens doors into our deeper, wiser self, calling us to step into the healing potential brought by the images and energies of our dreams.

## Guided meditation: The way of the dream

*When you wake up in the night or in the morning, be still and recall if you have been dreaming.*

*Don't rush out of bed.*

*Stay in your dreamlike state and linger with any dream image that comes to you.*

*Be still and let your dream unfold itself.*

*There might be one image that stays with you.*

*There might be the wisp of something that whispers to you from dream time.*

*Linger before your dream fades away.*

*If you have trouble reaching a dream you know is there, you may turn over in your bed, close your eyes and be still wait for a dream image to rise up and appear.*

*Bring your awareness to the one image that may stay with you as healing.*

*Anchor this image somewhere in your body.*

*Let it find home and become a part of your breathing self.*

*You may be called by this image to be with it, listen to it, let it guide your way.*

*Know too: You will not need to think of this image, for it will be there inside of you.*

*Trust your dream images, for they will guide you in subtle and important ways.*

## In your journal

Keep your journal next to your bed when you go to sleep.

Just before you close your eyes, open your journal to a blank page.

Take out your pen and write, in the middle of the page,

*Please bring me a dream.*

Leave your journal sitting open beside your bed.

When you awake and remember your dream, write it into your journal.

Give your dream a title. Miriam titled her dream: "A Gift from My Daughter"

Write a single word or phrase that captures what has stayed with you from your dream.

Draw any images that shine forth from your dream.

After you have written your dream into your journal, close your eyes and listen to what this dream is trying to tell you. Stay open to any message.

Sense the healing energy and let that energy breathe through your body.

As you read your journal in the months and years to come, you will see how your dreams have widened and deepened your awareness and brought healing to your life.

# 32.

## *I find my personal ritual of remembrance*

A YEAR AFTER BOB'S WIFE DOROTHY DIED, *he and his family gathered to create a memorial garden. They spent the day turning earth, enriching it, and planting rose bushes, the kind Dorothy loved. They planned to gather in that spot every year at the same time, a place where they can share loving memories of Dorothy and give their love an expression of beauty, carried on the scent of the roses.*

Gathering with family and friends to honor the one who has died keeps their spirit alive as they go on living through your memories. Someone has said we are alive as long as someone remembers us and says our name. It matters even when family is separated by distance and cannot gather, simply to know that wherever we are, we are acknowledging the anniversary of our shared love and loss.

There is a basic wisdom in the ritual of marking the time of death after one year has passed.

*I rarely went to synagogue. But in the year following my father's death, in honor of him, I went every week. I found it healing to observe the practice of standing when the Mourner's Prayer was recited. To stand each week with others who were mourning helped me feel less alone, helped me feel an unspoken bond with people I didn't know, people whose hearts held an ache like my own. To visibly and physically feel myself a part of the human circle of mourners made a profound difference to me.*

*To stop standing at the first anniversary of my father's death was a defining marker, a signal that an aspect of my grieving was over. That very act of not standing shifted the ground of my grief amid the community of grievers. It was now time for others to take their turn to stand weekly for the coming year. It was healing to see the wheel of life and death turning right before my eyes.*

We are all mourners, and we are all comforters for those whose turn it is to be counted in their grieving.

To know you are not alone, to feel you are part of the human cycle of birth and death can be a great solace. For me, it has made a profound difference. When my daughter died, I went through mourning in a very private way. Surely, there were loved ones around me, but there was little shared ritual. If I had known then of the solace offered by both religious and spiritual traditions, my grief may have been held and eased in the container of comfort that ritual offers.

Our rituals provide us some solid ground as we walk The Path of Grief. They don't have to be tied to any particular religion. They can be expressions of what we hold dear in our hearts. You can find within yourself what you need to mark that first anniversary and to continue to observe your beloved's death and life each year, expressing your love and remembrance.

*For my parents, I light a simple white candle in a simple holder on my table. I feel us gathered together around the table in spirit. This observance, this flickering light, helps me see their beloved faces before me as I honor both the struggles and joys of their lives.*

*Each year, on the anniversary of my daughter's death, I find a small piece of jewelry, a scarf or lovely journal. I choose what I sense Leslie would have chosen for me.*

*These gifts are special to me and wearing them helps me feel her loving presence all through the year.*

Our religious, spiritual, and personal rituals arising from our hearts can comfort and heal us in profound ways and help our spirits to touch and be touched by the spirits of our loved ones.

If your loss is too new or you feel you are too immersed in your grief to create a ritual, please give yourself the time you need to approach this step on your path.

The time will come from deep in the mystery of your being, perhaps when you least expect it, and you will know then what ritual calls to you. In your own time and in your own way, you will create your sacred ritual to honor and feel close to your loved one.

## Guided meditation: Receiving a ritual of remembrance

*Sit quietly with soft eyes, perhaps slowly closing them so that your attention can focus within.*

*Hold the intention to receive the ritual that will best express what sits in your heart.*

*Or you may wish to take an early morning walk in a park or along the beach, as you reflect upon the ritual that will be right for you and for your family.*

*In the quiet, let yourself wander in to those places you and your loved one enjoyed sharing.*

*Or perhaps a place that your loved one treasured visiting alone.*

*Perhaps a quiet garden, a bird sanctuary, or the beach, or a hilltop.*

*See the place as it appears before you.*

*Keep allowing your breathing to be gentle, even, steady—in and out—as you now see yourself in this place.*

*Know that you have come here to perform some sacred ritual to express your love and remembrance.*

*See and welcome whoever else might be there with you.*

*Or perhaps you are alone.*

*Feel and sense the presence of your loved one, perhaps in the light or in the stillness or in the sound of this place, or simply held in your heart.*

*Now, allow the ritual in your heart begin to unfold.*

*Take your time.*

*Let it unfold slowly, step by step. See what you are doing, perhaps alone, perhaps with others.*

*Are you planting a bush of flowers? Singing a song to your beloved's spirit? Flying a kite as he loved to do?*

*Or sitting in silent meditation or prayer?*

*Oftentimes, being able to unfold our ritual in the space of imagination is a preparation for carrying it into physical reality. Let yourself meditate on whether this is something you feel ready to do. Give yourself space and time to know when the time is right to carry forth the ritual you have received.*

*If you wish to create a ritual of remembrance and are hav-*

*ing difficulty, you can call upon your loved one in your med-
itation to come to help you.*

*Sitting with your eyes gently closed, come to your breath-
ing, become quiet in your body.*

*Whisper the name of your loved one and ask, "Please, my
beloved spouse. . .parent. . .child. . .sibling. . .friend. . . tell me
what you wish me to create as a ritual of remembrance for you.
I cannot do this myself and I so much want to create a ritual
that will show you my love and remembering. Please help me.
I am listening and waiting for your guidance."*

*And then, sitting quietly, breathing gently, wait until you
hear or see what your loved one brings to you.*

*Feel your gratitude for what you have received and feel the
gratitude of your loved one to be so loved by you.*

*If no ritual appears, simply know it is not time to receive
one. Know you have planted the seed and it will come in its
time.*

## *In your journal*

Sit quietly and recall the place you have entered to receive the ritual
you have asked for.

Write in detail all you have seen there and heard and sensed and
felt.

If your loved one has come to you in this place to bring the ritual
into your heart, allow the voice and presence of your love one speak to
you on the page.

Listen, hear, and write.

If it feels right, you might wish to draw the visual aspects of the ritual in detail, then listen: is there anything your heart wishes to say as

you present yourself at the ritual of remembrance?

Write it now so that it is there for you when the time comes to speak it aloud.

You may wish to speak aloud as you write, your hand and your heart joined in loving memory.

If no ritual appears to you, let yourself write your feelings of waiting.

Write into the place of unknowing from where we receive what we long for.

Write your longing or your fear of longing for a ritual with which to honor your loved one. Write of any obstacles, any blocks, you become aware of to receiving what you ask for.

# 33.

# *Life calls to me tenderly*

L IFE WILL CALL AGAIN. Unexpectedly, it will touch you from under the numbness, surge quietly like an underground stream, rising through the dark earth of your grief. Life will call quietly, come like a surprise. Perhaps in summer when a sudden rain touches your body and you tingle with a forgotten aliveness, or in the spring as you stop by a budding tree, or in fall as you watch an amber leaf letting go of its branch, or in winter as you lift your hand to touch the first snowfall. Childlike wonder will arise from somewhere inside you thought long dead and gone. Life will call again.

When life does call you back, you may resist, holding on to the deadness of your grief because you are afraid that if you come back to life, you may move too far away from your loved one.

*A few months after my daughter died, her little friend Sari, her eyes wide with disbelief, told me, "I used to be able to hear Leslie's voice, but I can't hear it anymore. It's gone far, far away. Where did it go?"*

Inevitably, the voice of our loved one becomes faint. Our sense of memories grows dim. We feel yet another sense of loss over the gradual disappearance of our sensory connections. When life calls to surprise our senses again, we may be reluctant to respond. Somehow, our aliveness follows the call of life. Grief teaches us this: When we feel our aliveness will be lost to us forever, life calls in the smallest of ways, touches deep into an aliveness we do not even know could be there. Out of our darkness rises a sense of reverence for life we have never felt before.

In reading through one of my journals, written more than a year after my daughter's death, I found this:

*"For the first time, today, I notice the flowers in the garden. Their beauty calls me out of myself after living in the dark for so long. I fill my vase with spring's new little yellow pansies and place them on my writing desk, where they shine in the sunlight. I feel the beauty of life in these spring flowers. Tears touch me with beauty in a way I never imagined sensing ever again and more deeply than I have ever known. As I behold the little yellow flowers. I feel alive again; I feel Leslie's hand become light touching my tears."*

As we feel the first stirrings of new life awakening in us, we are gently carried back toward life. We may invite a friend or two over for dinner and be surprised to find we enjoyed shopping, cooking simply, and setting the table again. We may find ourselves carrying out our daily, ordinary tasks more caringly, in a meditative way. We may notice we are paying closer attention now, taking nothing for granted, aware of small living moments we had overlooked before. We are touched and slowed to take in how the lettuce glistens, how the summer tomato bursts with deep red juice, how the wine glass sparkles. All glowing moments of precious life sitting upon our table.

As we emerge from our deep grief called into the light and colors

of life, we may feel more alive than ever before. As we are called to
new beginnings and new hope, we feel our senses heightened and our
devotion to all life renewed, deeper than ever before. We realize we
have come back to life, guided by the light of the spirit of our loved
one, this light now suffusing everything around us.

Again, from my journal, written two years after Leslie's leaving:

*"I look up at the sky. It is dawn. I see the morning star. It is
neither day nor night. It is both end and beginning. I welcome the
pale, morning light of the sun into my heart.*

*In this light, I feel the blessing to go on. And I sense my daughter
also goes on in this same light. I bless the day. I am comforted and
grateful to be part of precious and fragile life."*

It is not easy to come back to life, to accept the grace of new beginnings. You have lived a long time in grief and there is a place in you,
in each of us, that will go on mourning. Loss is pitched deep in the
dark soil of our lives. Our sense of loss becomes a permanent part of
who we are. But so is the light calling us back to life. Somehow, it is
our nature to go on holding both, darkness and light, brokenness and
wholeness, death and life. It is all a part of our being human, and it is
all a holy mystery, this life and this death.

## *Guided meditation: Life calls to me*

*Sit comfortably. Be still. Listen.*

*Sense if you can feel a stirring deep within you, moving,
pulsing, breathing with the subtle energies of life.*

*Stay open, breathing in and out.*

*Sense in this moment how life is calling you back from the
frozen silence of your grief.*

*Listen quietly and let yourself be touched by whatever is*

*alive for you in this moment.*

*What is it that touches you with the movement of life?*

*From within you and around you?*

*Feel and sense life returning, stirring through your body, your breathing, sense the breath of life touching you.*

*Know how you are breathing the breath of life being breathed.*

*Take the time to feel life's energies circulating through your body, through your breathing, through every organ, through your blood stream.*

*Feel life lifting your head to the vast heavens, to the clear sky, to the golden sun.*

*Feel life lifting your arms as well to bring down the blessings of life upon you.*

*Do you feel reluctant to come alive again? Do you feel a rebirth of excitement?*

*Do you feel the pendulum swing back and forth, from reluctance to excitement, and back again?*

*If so, know it is natural for the pendulum of these feelings to swing back and forth.*

*Let yourself move from not wanting to step forth into life and wanting to, allow and embrace the life wrapped in each feeling.*

*As you are touched by the flow of life, you may experience an ache, a keen missing of the aliveness you shared with your loved one.*

*Know how this ache is a sacred memory sitting in the sanctuary of your heart.*

*Open from your deep self to express your gratitude for life returning, stirring within you even as you may be reluctant to enter its flow.*

*Feel how to sense yourself touched by life after being numb and lost is a blessing.*

*May you bow your head to your heart, grateful to feel even a drop of new dear life calling to you, even if you do not yet know how to live with it.*

## In your journal

Write in your journal how you sense life calling you in small ways.

What is different? What is changing?

How do you respond to this call?

With a tear of longing for the life you shared with your loved one?

With a smile of childlike wonder to see the sunlight on the grass?

To see the cat rolling over? To hear the stranger beside you humming?

With both tears and smiles, as you hold your sadness of loss in one hand and your sense of sacred life in the other?

Write in your journal for 15 minutes without stopping.

Write about the ways you feel touched by life during the day.

What does life returning to you move you toward?

Making a dinner for friends or family?

Planting flowers? Serving at a soup kitchen?

Attending a new class? Listening to or playing some music? Or. . . ?

Write about what you feel called to by life.

Perhaps you can make a commitment in your journal to what you feel most moved to carry through with in the coming days and weeks.

Allow life calling to write to you Allow loss to write to you.

Write it all, each feeling as it appears. Life calling grief, asking to be felt.

Let it all be there.

If it feels right, you may write on two facing pages:

On one page: Life is calling. I listen. I hear. I allow. I write.

On the facing page: Loss is calling. I listen. I hear. I allow. I write.

I write each wave as it moves through me.... all that is now part of my being alive.

# 34.

## *What do life and death mean to me?*

I KNEW MY GRANDMOTHER as the softest, most loving presence in my life. She put love all over me. I still remember how I saw in her smile her full love for me. And then, suddenly, she was gone. I never again went to her house after school to sit with her while she taught me how to sew, not just stitching the fabric, but all the torn places in my little life.

After her sudden passing when I was eight years old, I remember worrying that my mother and father might die suddenly in the middle of the night or while I was away at school.

With adulthood and its inevitable losses, the fears of loss we faced in childhood can come rolling back across time. Many of you know your own feelings of aloneness and loss, know how early experiences of loss profoundly shape your current images of death and entwine them with feelings of dread or comfort, depending on how your grief was held for you in childhood. These feelings become deeply embedded in the survival part of our brains, penetrating our sense of what dying and death mean. Many of us are in touch with reliving childhood traumatic grief in our current adult losses.

We can, however, find a possible way to see, and feel, and sort the past from the present. When we open our senses into the realm of imagination, we have the opportunity to discover something other and beyond our known fears. In the space of imagination, we can open a door to some deeper wisdom that can sit beside us and hold our frightening early beliefs, hovering like a dark cloud over the present. In the open possibilities of imagination, we are often surprised to find what waits to be discovered by us, beyond the constricting territories of our life-long, habitual fears.

Here, I share with you the opening to a healing way of beholding death. In this experience, I guided myself in the same way I offer to anyone who comes to me for help with old, traumatic, dreaded images of death.

*I close my eyes and stand before a door marked with the word "Death."*

*When I open the door of death, I see the figure of Kwan Yin, the Buddhist Mother of Mercy. She sits quietly, waiting to welcome all those who pass through the doorway.*

*Beside her sits a skeleton, bathed, clean to the bone, radiating bright light from its very marrow. I know this to be Death.*

*Between them sits an old clay bowl, broken, its cracks filled with shimmering gold.*

*Kwan Yin places this bowl into my outstretched hands. Without words, I have been given a cracked bowl, mended with golden light to carry with me on my journey through loss and love.*

*I know this to be the Blessing Bowl of my heart. I will always carry this bowl of golden, healing light. It will bring a glow of quiet to my cracked and broken heart. I will lift the bowl into my hands and reach it toward the broken hearts of others who are passing through. With this bowl, I will bless the day. With this simple bowl, I will remember to say, "I am sorry" and "thank you," without waiting for a tomorrow that may not come.*

*The presence of the wise and merciful Kwan Yin and the skeleton of Death sitting together have melted my fear at what awaited me behind the door of "Death." Seeing them as companions opened my heart to a reality of how death and mercy go hand in hand, caring for and opening the heart and bringing tender light to its cracks.*

*With my eyes still closed, I brought that frightened six-year-old girl, who had suddenly lost the refuge that was her beloved grandmother. The little girl stood with me and with Death and Kwan Yin. I let her hold and feel the cracked bowl, which was hers as well. I felt the cracked bowl to be our heart of grief, the crack remaining, only now touched with the gold of loving-kindness and understanding. I placed the bowl into my heart and hers and called it a Blessing Bowl, out of which to give and receive blessings.*

I do not believe the little one will ever be fully free of her dread of Death, but she is no longer alone.

Eternal mercy goes with her in the Blessing Bowl of her heart.

## *Guided meditation: Opening the Door of Death*

*Take time to sit quietly with your breathing until you feel ready to enter the space of imagination where anything is possible, where you can be anywhere, with anyone, at any time.*

*Now, breathe out three times, counting backward from*

*three to two to one.*

*When you reach one, know you have reached the oneness of your wise and eternal self.*

*When you reach one, breathe back to zero.*

*See the zero become a golden circle.*

*Step through the golden circle and breathe a long breath, leading you to a door.*

*See yourself standing in front of the door.*

*See what the door is made of and see that it is marked with the word "Death."*

*Open the door and look inside.*

*Be aware of all you see and hear, sense, and feel.*

*If you are frightened, close the door and know you can come back another time.*

*Or, in the space of your imagination, call out for the help of a someone to be with you.*

*See who comes to be beside you, a friend, a guide.*

*Stay aware of your body and breathing as you open the door.*

*What do you find when you open the Door of Death?*

*Take your time to be with whoever and whatever waits there to greet you and guide you.*

*Perhaps a wise and eternal presence who wants to say something to you, to give you something to carry with you on your way.*

*Perhaps you wish to release something into the hands of the wise one.*

*Take all the time you need in this space.*

*Perhaps what waits for you behind the door is frightening. If so, turn and close the door, knowing you can return another time and bring protection with you.*

*May what awaits you behind the Door of Death hold you in the wisdom of your eternal Self. May the blessing below be yours to carry in your heart:*

*When I come to open the Door of Death,*

*may I receive comfort in what greets me.*

*May I be able to see deep into birth, and life, and death.*

*May I receive a blessing from behind the Door of Death, a blessing for my heart to carry on my grief journey to help me live my life with compassion, for myself and all beings.*

## *In your journal*

Take your time and write your journey to the Door of Death.

Write in detail all you see, and sense, and feel in the space behind the door Keep writing with pen on page until you are finished recording your journey.

As you write, do you have any further questions, anything further to receive?

Contemplate the ways in which what you have received from behind the Door of Death in any ways helps you to go on. Write.

Before you prepare to close your journal, sit for a while with eyes softly closed.

Do you hear a blessing being given to you?

If so, open your journal and write it.

Take what wisdom and healing you have received and place it in your heart.

Write the blessing that is brought to you.

Sit for a while breathing quietly what now sits within you.

Is there anything more you wish to write?

# 35.

# *Out of this darkness, creativity is born*

OUR DEFINITIONS OF CREATIVITY ARE OFTEN LIMITED: We automatically think of best-selling authors, successful visual artists, or musicians. In a deeper way, creativity has to do with our living in the flow of creation. Creative living springs from our inner impulse and capacity to receive from life and give to life. When we enter on The Path of Grief, a sense of overwhelming loss can dull our sense of the flow of life. For some time, we live in the empty spaces between what was and what is yet to be. The call of life is muted, lost to us, sometimes for a very long time. Within and all around us, the world seems without color, pale, without life. We are lost to life and not yet found.

As you live in in-between spaces of grief, as you go about your day, you may begin to sense the colors of the faint voice of your desires, Life whispering, calling to you. As you write in your journal, clean your house, go for a walk, or have a conversation, you may hear your inner voice speak and you may begin to sense a stirring in the creative well-springs of your spirit. Here, there abides your healing, your sensing the glimmering forth of an ember of life force. As you listen to what stirs deep within, you can begin to follow, to make choices of how to go forward into life once again, at first to choose life in very small ways.

As you listen down into life gently stirring, you may find yourself arranging something as simple as a bowl of fruit or washing and slicing some fresh vegetables for a lunch. You may find yourself newly alive in the way you say "Hello" to someone, or look at someone and smile, or look into the eyes of a beloved pet. This life flowing from your heart can transform the simplest of everyday gestures into creative acts that touch and honor the life of all beings and all things. As you make these seemingly small creative acts of daily life, you notice you are coming back to life, only this time with a new sense of treasuring what is alive in front of your eyes. This is what I call the art of creative living. Somehow, along the journey of grief, out of the depths of loss, we are brought to a reverence of life we never before knew. We go on living in a paradox of knowing both the ache of loss and the love for all that lives.

If we pay close attention to the voice within, we can access the well-springs of love and find ourselves touched by life moving *through our* grief. As we reawaken to life, things that never called to us before may suddenly surprise and excite us.

*After his brother's death, Simon spent much of his time in the park on his favorite bench by the lake and began to take a keen interest in the birds nesting there. He watched them for hours, intrigued by their habits, moved by their beauty. He bought a pair of field glasses and several books. For the first time in his life, Simon became an avid bird watcher.*

*A few years after her young son died of leukemia, Linda began volunteering in the nursery at the local hospital one day a week. She cradled and nurtured premature babies, reentering her own life as her holding, touching, and rocking infused life into those newborns.*

After my daughter died, I begin to write in a journal, searching for the words to express my unspeakable loss. I had no interest in writing before Leslie's death, but after years and years of writing in my journals, the door opened to writing this book.

Soul wings somehow form out of the ashes of death and loss, lifting our spirit into a never-before-experienced intense devotion to life that stirs the deep well of our creative living. Out of our despair, life comes to us with a poignant sense of purpose that wants nothing more than to bless and protect all that contains the breath of life. This is the paradox our grief journey asks us to live with: the knowing of the deepest pain of loss and the deepest love of life.

## *Guided meditation: I drink from the well*

*Come to your place to sit. Make yourself comfortable.*

*Close your eyes. Focus your attention on your breathing.*

*As you breathe out, see yourself standing at a deep well of clear water.*

*Find a silver cup beside the well, tied to a long golden cord.*

*Pick up the cup and lower it into the water.*

*Know this to be the well of your heart.*

*Draw the cup up out of the water and drink from it.*

*As you drink, sense how clear and clean the water, sense how the water is refreshing and renewing your heart.*

*Sense and feel the movement of your heart's desire being*

*watered.*

*Feel with your whole body and spirit what it is that you want to water in life.*

*See yourself receiving from and giving to life in small ways.*

*Be aware of any pleasure of aliveness coming to your body and spirit.*

*You may find yourself slowing down to notice the autumn leaves floating to the ground, or smile at someone standing in line with you, or delight feeling the warm sun on your face.*

*Know how, in these small ways of sensing sacred Life all around you, of holding life as sacred, you are bearing witness, treasuring, affirming, and being part of creation.*

*May your grief open your heart to how sacred life is.*

*May you feel called to tend the sacredness of all life.*

*May you bow your head to your heart, the deep well of love and creativity.*

*May you carry your heart as a Blessing Bowl to the sacredness life.*

*If you are not yet ready to drink from the well of your heart, if the well is dry with grief, know that the water is deep underground, waiting to come to you when it is your time to drink from the waters of new life.*

## *In your journal*

Sit with a clear glass of water beside you and your journal.

Look at the water and let it become the water drawn from the well of your heart.

Drink the water and sense the living water stirring within you—a pulsation of life—no matter how slight. Let the pulsation slowly spread through your body.

Take your time to sense any desire that is stirred, no matter how small.

Let this desire write itself onto your journal page.

Be still. Listen again. Write whatever arises.

Is there any commitment you wish to make to a desire you feel toward a creative gesture, no matter how small? If so, write your commitment in your journal.

For example: This week, as autumn turns the leaves to brown, I will walk in the park. I will stop and stand with one tree and really see the colors of the leaves. In this way, I will be a part of life turning, creation always turning.

If you are not ready to feel the pulsing of aliveness move through you, sense and accept the truth of that. Let that move through your body and write onto the blank page of your journal.

# 36.

# *I listen to the voice of aloneness*

A s you move through grief, you learn to live in your new aloneness. Slowly, you learn to live through long nights, be in an empty house, face your terrors, and accept the feelings of emptiness as well as the tears, heartache, sorrow, and painful memories as they each open in you. As your grief slowly weaves aloneness into the fabric of your life, you come to acknowledge being alone is now an intrinsic part of who you are. Before, there was ongoing relationship, companionship, a comfortable presence; now, it has vanished. This is your new reality to face, your new state of being. At first, you may turn away from your aloneness, afraid you can't bear it. As you come to accept your aloneness as an inevitable part of your grief, as you sit with it, let it teach you, allow it the time it needs, you come to know who you are, now. As you accept the way things are now, in time, with patience and great kindness to yourself, you will find a place for aloneness to sit with you in your new life and discover it as a deep part of your inner home.

For a long time after the death of my daughter, aloneness was the excruciating cutting of a sharp knife into my solar plexus. Aloneness hurt that much. After journeying along the path of loss and love, aloneness gradually transformed to become like the stucco houses of Greece, painted white, inside and out, unadorned, bare, open to the vast blue of sky and sea, open to the breeze and sun entering through open doors and windows. Here, my aloneness is held in an atmosphere of calm and quiet. I sit in the stillness of white. In this space, I let my aloneness come, speak to me, weep with me, and be in quiet reverie, as I open to whatever appears within these walls.

A woman I know senses her solitary inner place that grew out of her grief as a warm, dark space—a silent cave in a thick, quiet forest. This cave of her imagination sits inside her as she sits inside of it.

My white, bare, quiet Greek room sits inside of me as I sit inside of it, always open, always there to come to, to sit in, to be with the silence of *alone.*

For a long time after my daughter died, I was terrified to be alone, to be only with myself, terrified of falling into a black hole of non-being. Who was I if I was alone and without the one who was flesh of my flesh? I was no one, the blank of alone. I simply did not know *how* to be alone. Being alone with my grief, alone with myself, was not possible for me during those trembling times after my child's death. Only very slowly was I able to sit down beside my shock, and terror, and frozen tears, face them, and give them the tenderness they needed.

*Slowly, very slowly*, my fear of the deadly quiet and my terror of being alone transformed into a sense of healing solitude. Gradually, my anxiety came to rest in the healing power of stillness. Over time, I realized the quiet white-walled alone space of my Greek sanctuary had grown larger than my terror and could hold it in safety and compassion.

*Slowly, over time,* I came to know aloneness well enough to step inside for longer and longer periods of time. I came to know and value the qualities of aloneness—the lingering quiet, the timelessness, the sacred stillness—while I did the dishes, washed and dried the lettuce, listened to music or to the rain outside my window. Sometimes I would lie down and close my eyes, not to sleep, but to enter the dark comfort of aloneness, to discover who I was in that space, in that moment, to open and learn how to just *be* with whatever I was truly feeling, and to gently accept whatever was arising out of my aloneness.

This space of aloneness, discovered in my deep grief, has slowly become a sacred space I can enter to encounter and witness my true being and listen to my true voice.

Now, being alone is like mindfully walking to the center of a labyrinth, to the center of myself, stepping into the still center of my inner home, where I can find the healing stillness I need in my life.

Grief was what first brought me to my white-walled still Greek house, and now, after so many years, this white-walled place of solace still invites me in, waiting to greet and hold the innocent inner aliveness of all that wants to be known and felt in my life. On the journey of grief, out of the agony of aloneness came the solace of aloneness, came the root of my meditation practice.

When along our journey of grief, as we come to create a balance in which we are connected both to our inner selves and to those we are closest to, we will not feel isolated when we are alone, nor wanting alone space when we are with others. When we are alone, we will know we are always connected meaningfully with others, and when we are with others we know we can always have our sacred time of solitude.

## Guided meditation: Finding healing
## in the stillness

*Sit quietly in your space of solitude.*

*In a favorite chair, a meditation cushion, atop your bed, prone on a carpet, on your comfortable sofa.*

*Give yourself this gift of time to still your outer life, to go gently within.*

*Sense the quiet in your room touching the quiet within your body, heart, and spirit.*

*Allow an image of your quiet space to open: See how it looks and feels.*

*Perhaps it is a serene house overlooking the sea, a silent cave, a mountain top, a crystal lake.*

*Let your place come to you and let yourself come to it.*

*Know that this inner sanctuary is yours to return to again and again.*

*Your place to come to find stillness for whatever is inside of you.*

*Let your body release into the rhythm of your breathing, let stillness breathe you.*

*In this space, there is nothing to do, only to feel and follow your own rhythm, the rhythm of your breath, the rhythm of your feelings, of your body and spirit.*

*In reverie, let yourself drift on the stream of your awareness.*

*Be with what arises and is present here, now.*

*Let your exhalation become long enough to carry you any-where it wants to take you.*

*See where you come to: Is it a place in nature? Or some-where else?*

*Know this as your place to carry your aloneness to.*

*See and know what opens for you in this place of your*

*aloneness.*

*A meditative peace; a shedding of tears; a deep, loving smile; the hum of a melody.*

*Perhaps despair, sitting heavy in your chest, perhaps a plea for healing.*

*In your place of aloneness, let yourself be surprised by whatever may come.*

*Sink deep into contemplation into a waking dream.*

*Let yourself be free of doing, simply be,*

*Feel what is there in your sanctuary of aloneness.*

*Let yourself sense how when you give over to your alone time and place your time with your deep self, you come to where there is no clock, no time, only "being time."*

*You can be in your sanctuary as long as you need and leave in your own rhythm.*

## *In your journal*

Write your experience of journeying to your place of aloneness.

Write for 15 minutes without stopping.

Write in detail about the place you came to.

Write in detail about all you saw, heard, sensed, and felt.

Be in touch with your sense of how it is for you on the path of your grief, to come to this sanctuary for your aloneness.

Write about your aloneness, all of its colors and sounds, all of it.

Write of any consolation the sanctuary you have found brings to your aloneness.

When you are finished writing, take some time and sense:

Does anything else need to be seen, felt, written about?

Ask your aloneness. . .listen for the answer. . .write.

# 37.

# *The mysteries of life and death are entwined*

I T IS THE BEGINNING OF SPRING, perhaps April. You decide to take a morning walk or an early evening stroll. You notice the air is balmy. You look around and are surprised to see the grass glowing purple and yellow with crocuses and daffodils. You look up to see dogwood and cherry trees bursting with new buds. Fragrance fills the air, birdsong filters through treetops, and every one of your senses awakens. You are lighthearted, your steps buoyant. By some amazing grace, you are stirred with a sense of happiness!

And then, suddenly, something pulls you back: A familiar sadness overtakes you, and, once again, you are aware of a deep ache of loss in your heart. This unexpected feeling surprises you in this moment of happiness, but you know it well: It is the familiar ache of loss, the echo of your grief, now side-by-side with the glow of the sudden beauty brought by Spring. You continue your walk with both the thrill of new life and the ache of life lost stirring within you.

T.S. Eliot called April the cruelest month. Perhaps he meant it is the most poignant of months, for in April the mysteries of birth and the mysteries of death come together. In nature, in the seasons, in our heart, these two currents of life course simultaneously. While the color and beauty of Spring takes our breath away, we know it to be short-lived, we know the blossoming and flowering will give way to wilt and death, and so we feel the fragility of beauty and life itself. When we are walking The Path of Grief and it is April, we will be both surprised by the sudden joy of aliveness and the sense of impermanence, of our loss being side-by-side.

Many of us are cut off from the cycles of birth and death. Those who still live close to nature—in the country, on the farm—are fortunate to see animals mate, give birth, and die; watch the earth bear fruit, multiply, then lie fallow until new seeds are sown. The religious sect known as The Shakers reportedly set large cradles near their kitchen fireplaces, where their dying elders rested and were warmed alongside the smaller cradles of the newborns. Some still dig their own graves, make their own coffins, birth their own babies at home—their daily lives a part of the perpetual turning of the wheel of life and death.

By moving farther away from nature, we have lost touch with the keen understanding that, while every birth and death in our own life is unique and sacred to us, we are all, collectively, participants in the ever-changing larger currents of life and death. We *are* part of a cosmic order and are not isolated in the experience of our own loss.

I have a friend, a middle-aged woman, who has often had the strange misfortune—or fortune—of encountering little wounded birds on the streets of her town. As long as she can remember, she has noticed birds with broken wings, broken legs, and has never been able to pass them by without scooping them up, taking them home, nesting them into old shoe boxes, and tending them carefully.

Some of them heal and fly away, but most die and are buried by my friend.

The other day, my friend told me she was walking along her street when she came upon a small, yellow bird that had fallen out of a tree. Its leg appeared to be injured. She took it home, settled it into a shoe-box of a nest on her back porch and gave it water and breadcrumbs. When she saw it was sitting contentedly in the nest, she phoned me and said: "You know, I've been thinking, it doesn't seem right that I brought this bird home. Birds belong in nature, and it seems to me now that nature can take care of its own better than I can. I want to take the bird back to the park and set it down under a tree. If it doesn't survive, then nature will be acting in its own way: Not everything in nature survives. I no longer want to interrupt nature's cycle of life and death. You know, when I was younger, I never thought to leave a wounded bird to fare for itself, of letting nature take care of its own. But since my father has died, my mother has grown old, and I am aging, I'm more accepting of death. I think I am learning to accept that death is a part of life and not foreign to it. So, yes, I think I'll take the bird to the park and return it to the place where it has lived and will die. I think what matters is that the bird be allowed to stay in its home in nature. I know what matters most to me, at this point in my life, is that I be allowed to live in my own place, in *my* true nature."

My friend told me later that when she had donned her coat and returned to the porch to get the bird, she found the shoebox nest empty: The bird had spread its wings and flown back to its home, had itself reentered nature's cycle, and left its helper alone to contemplate the mystery of the coming and going, of her own living and dying.

## *Guided meditation: I behold the passing moments*

While you sit quietly in meditation, ponder the mystery of birth and death.

Whatever the season, be aware of it as part of a greater cycle of seasons.

Be aware of a cosmic, turning wheel, continually moving from life to death to rebirth and on and on.

As you envision the people you know and love, see their place in the cycle of life and death.

Look into their faces: Are they shining with the glow of youth or lined and touched with the softened glow of age?

See your own place in life's cycle.

Look in the mirror and know where you are along this turning wheel.

Look into the lines on your face, your songlines, sensing how they tell the story of your life.

Touch the lines on your face, trace them with your finger, and, no matter if you are young or old, know how these lines, the lines of your body and spirit, are being turned and sculpted on the wheel of life and death.

Now bring your loved one who has died to your mind and heart.

Know how their death is the natural companion to their life.

Sense and feel your loved one's departure as part of the ceaseless and mysterious process that all living belongs to.

Sense the reality of all things coming and going, being born, ceasing to live, becoming light of spirit.

If your loved one has died prematurely, sit quietly as you

*ponder how this may not feel like a natural ending at all, may indeed live in you as a tragic ending.*

*Be aware how this tragic death of your loved one is also surrounded by a sense of mystery that is beyond your understanding.*

*For a moment, feel yourself living with acceptance of the ever-turning wheel of life and death.*

*Watch the wheel turn, feel it turning, feel each season, each life beginning and coming to its end.*

*Sense the reality of all things coming and going, the little bird, the clouds, the moon, your loved one, your breathing in, and your breathing out.*

*Allow each feeling to arise in your awareness.*

*Feel the sadness, helplessness, anger, poignancy, quiet yearning, sorrow, deep grief, sense of awe, sweet memories.*

*Breathe acceptance, as you remain with the full turning of your feelings.*

*Be with whatever arises.*

*Give each feeling its time to appear, to move in you and through you.*

*Return to your breathing until another feeling enters your awareness.*

*Be with the whole cycle of your feelings.*

*Be with whatever surges as you sit with the wheel of life and death.*

*Watching it turn, feeling it turn, feeling each season, each life beginning and ending.*

*Notice your breath come and go; watch the clouds come and go.*

*Hear the sounds come and go. Know how you, too, are a*

*part of all that comes and goes.*

*As you journey along your path of grief, know how it may not be possible just now to accept that your loved one's death is a part of the turning of the wheel of life and death. Along your way, may you come to a time when you are able to hear yourself whisper: I will allow and accept everything I feel, as it moves in and out. I will not pick and choose.*

## *In your journal*

As you meditate on the cycle of life and death, on all things coming and going, arising and fading away, write your thoughts and feelings as you contemplate the comings and goings of your life, of life.

Let your journal be a witness to your feelings to each ephemeral breath, to each passing thought, to each feeling, as it comes and goes.

Take your time write as a thought, or feeling, or body sense arises.

Then, put your pen down, sit again, breathe, wait, be with whatever comes, write.

Let your writing be a meditation.

May you breathe gently.

May you smile a soft *thank you* for this precious moment of life here, now, that *will* pass like a cloud, but has not been taken for granted.

Write your gratitude onto a blank page, breathe, write slowly.

Breathing, hear yourself say: I am here. I am here for this moment of life. I am here. I am grateful.

# 38.

## *The voice of my loneliness guides me*

LONELINESS AND SOLITUDE ARE NOT THE SAME. Solitude opens to an inner space, where we can meet ourselves in the very moment. Loneliness is different. Loneliness, if it goes on too long, does not open us to ourselves. The loneliness that can emerge in grief can close us down and confine our living space.

Loneliness can build a fence around our life. Loneliness can say, "I don't have any friends. They were all my husband's friends. There's no future for me. There's nothing I'm excited about. Life is boring, empty. No one wants me. I am lonely." Loneliness that can take us over in our grief journey can cut us off from our movement into life.

If, however, we really listen to the voice of our loneliness, we are able to hear another voice wrapped deep inside of it. It is the voice of our longing. If we listen closer to, "I no longer have any friends," we may hear, "I want friends. I am lonely for friends. I long for them." If we listen carefully to, "There's no future for me. There's nothing I'm excited about," we may hear, "I want a future, my future. I want to feel excited again." You are perhaps reluctant to hear the voice of your longing because you believe you will be disloyal to your loved one, who is leaving or is now gone. You are not alone, for it is in our nature for grief and loyalty to become entwined. Grief is no longer the pure feeling of loss but is now entwined with the fear that, if we go on, in doing so, we will be disloyal to our loved one.

*Charlotte came to see me after her husband of many years died. She shared how lonely her life was—how her work, her social life, and her creative life were all at a standstill. As we sat together, Charlotte wept and gradually gave voice to the longing wrapped in her loneliness. She wanted to see her friends. She wanted to find expression for the creativity stirring within her on the path of her grief journey. She was reluctant to share any of this with me, feeling that even to speak the words of her desire would be a betrayal of her beloved husband. I told Charlotte that I sensed her standing on a bridge in her life now, fearing to cross over toward new life. She closed her eyes and saw herself standing on the middle of a bridge, between her past and her future.*

*In her imagination, she stood there, desolate, lonely, and longing. Crying, she said goodbye to her husband. She told him how hard it was to leave, but that it was time to listen to and follow her heart along the bridge of her life.*

*She watched as her husband waved goodbye to her and began to sail away in a boat, giving her permission to go as well. She sensed that her husband had been waiting for her to be ready to go so that he could also be released to his own journey. Charlotte watched her hus-*

*band sail away. Crying softly, she turned from the shore of her former life and began to walk across the bridge toward an unknown future on the far shore.*

*When she came to the middle of the bridge, I asked her what she was able to see on the far side. "I see a bed of leaves waiting for me, waiting for me to come and rest," she said. "I need to do that before I can go any further into the future. It is a lovely soft bed. I am so touched to see it there, waiting for me." Tears of gratitude welled up in Charlotte's eyes and a whisper of a smile appeared.*

*After this journey of imagination, for the next few weeks, whenever Charlotte needed, she came to her bed of leaves to be with her missing of her husband, with the waves of her grief, with the budding of her desire.*

*Charlotte wrote in her journal each day about what it was like for her to be in this new land, on the far side of the bridge of her loss. Then, after two weeks, closing her eyes and entering the space of her imagination, she found herself getting up from the bed of leaves. She stood, facing the far side of the bridge, the side that held new life for her. She knew it was her time to cross the bridge and follow her desire.*

*In the coming weeks and months, Charlotte joined an art class. Her first painting was of the bridge and of herself on the bed of leaves. Not only did Charlotte begin to paint for the first time in her life, she made new friends and felt a renewed spark of excitement to be living new life while, at the same time, cherishing her memories of her husband and carrying his essence on with her. She spoke of how she felt herself seeing with his eyes as well as her own. She spoke of smiling when sunset came and felt him beside her on the grass where they used to sit. Charlotte crossed the bridge carrying her loving devotion to her husband with her.*

## *Guided meditation: Crossing the bridge*

*Sit quietly, breathe in and out. Rest in the pause the in-between place.*

*As you breathe, come to the inner space of your imagination.*

*Breathe a long exhalation and find yourself standing at the foot of a bridge between your past and your future.*

*Standing on the ground of your old life, prepare to step onto the bridge.*

*Ask yourself: What do I need to do before I move on?*

*How do I begin to leave my old life, my old country, how do I go on?*

*Is someone from your old life standing on the side of the bridge you are getting ready to leave?*

*What might you need to say to them or them to you so that you can go on?*

*Do they give you anything to carry with you into your future?*

*Where do you place this gift to carry with you as you prepare to go on to the bridge?*

*What might you wish to give them before you turn to go?*

*Now, see the one you are with, either physically or in spirit, turning to go.*

*Sense yourself alone with your life as you prepare to enter and cross the bridge.*

*See yourself step onto the bridge and begin to cross it.*

*When you come to the middle, stop and look back, then look ahead.*

*Take your time.*

*Is there anything you wish to lift out of your body?*

*Something you do not want to carry with you?*

*If so, reach into yourself and lift out whatever it is you do not want to take with you, as you continue to cross the bridge.*

*Be aware of what it means for your life to let this go.*

*Cast it over the side of the bridge and let the water carry it away.*

*Begin walking across the bridge toward your future.*

*What do you see and sense waiting for you?*

*Sense how the breath of life instills in you a trust that what you need, and desire waits for you on the other side of the bridge. Breathe in the clear air surrounding you.*

*If you cannot yet see a glimpse of what awaits you, know that you can keep returning to your bridge.*

*Take your time to face your fears of going on, perhaps your fear that nothing will be there for you at the other side of the bridge.*

*Trust that when you are ready, life will hear your longing to enter a new beginning and guide you along the path of loss and love to enter and move along your bridge.*

*And then you will say, "Thank you, life, thank you bridge of my life, for carrying me on my journey through grief to this place."*

*Until then, know the time will come when you are ready. If you feel you need more time, honor this feeling, knowing you can return to this meditation whenever you hear the call to come to the bridge toward your future.*

## *In your journal*

Turn to two blank facing pages.

On one side, let your loneliness or fear have their voice.

Ask what it needs, how it wants to express itself.

Write down what you hear.

As you sit with your loneliness or fear and write what it says, listen closely for any desire wrapped within these feelings.

If your feelings speak about what is missing, what is wrong, what is not as it should be, what will not be there for you, let yourself notice how this may be a way of saying what is wanted, desired, and truly longed for.

On the other side of the page, write down what loneliness or fear desire: friendship, calm, new ideas, a meaningful project, a new sense of purpose.

Whatever you long for, honor this as a sacred longing life is calling you toward.

You may choose to write with colored pencils that reflect the colors of your desire.

Pay close attention to where your desire sits in your body; place your hand there.

Feel the way it sits in your body—sense, listen, write.

Ask your desire: Please guide me, show me the next steps. Write what you hear.

# 39.

## *Offering up my sounds of sorrow*

FIRST, THERE IS ONLY EMPTY SILENCE, the muted sighs of grief, soundless tears. It takes time for the music of life to come back to us, for a real song to rise out of our hearts, one that isn't forced as we try to belong to life again. For a long time, we may live in a numbing silence of barely audible existence.

Sounds of life may be heard as far away, unreachable.

A year after my daughter died, someone said to me, "It will take time. Time is the great healer."

Though it was meant to help, "It will take time" was not something I believed. I believed my tears were endless. I didn't want to be healed by time. I didn't want time or anything else to separate me from my golden-haired child: My tears and my deep sorrow were lingering threads of connection to her.

As I continued on my journey through grief, I learned tears were not the only connection with my daughter. Along the way, my broken heart came to know the myriad of ways in which my connection to Leslie endured and guided me toward renewed songs of life. Just as journeying into new lands affects and changes us, our time spent on the Path of Grief does, eventually transforming us. There are many stops along the way.

In this land of grief, you may not have any tears, only numbness, a sense of deadness that is itself a form of crying, dry crying. Tears won't fall, or when they begin, they seem to never stop. Here, in the land of grief, pain can feel like the actual, physical cut of a blunt knife; or like the pain of reaching out and not finding, fingers aching to touch; of speaking and there is no longer anyone there to hear us. We feel swept into an endlessly desolate place, without any capacity or desire to move on.

Carried by the movement of time and mercy, you may find yourself glimpsing and then crossing a threshold, touched by the return of the pulsations of life. Here, our tears may breathe through our numbness. Numbness may, in time, soften into the soothing of a breathing silence. In this land, there may come a sense of silence that you may carry within you that is different from the empty silence of numbness. This is the silence that stirs in us as we sense being embraced and comforted by an invisible, and yet palpable, and pulsating mystery that embraces and comforts our grief and sustains us as we move along our journey.

Over the years, through my journey of grief, I have never forgotten the sense of a holy silence that surrounded my daughter as her spirit left her body. That holy silence filled with and touching my daughter with a great love has continued to abide, always waiting for the door of my heart to become quiet and open to its presence.

How to describe this silence that is neither dark nor despairing, even in death? The silence of light filtering through a pine forest; the stillness of the star-filled heavens over the endless sea; the empty, spacious silence of deep meditation. And, more than any words can convey, in my heart I know this to be the awesome silence surrounding the mystery of life and death. This is a silence beyond any question or answer, beyond words or intellect. It is what I have come to call the Great Silence of the Great Love without end, within and all around, the mystery of existence. The silence of being, of creation, that surrounds the being born, the living, and the dying of all beings.

When this vast silence comes to us, when this great love opens deep within, we will still cry, still feel grief, and still feel lost in darkness. But now, we are touched by some new stirring, of a sense of the sacred deep inside and all around us. As our eyes open wide to look out into the universe, searching this mystery, we may find a slight smile upon our lips. A smile that understands, beyond words, what it is that walks and travels with us now alongside our grief.

In this land, out of this great silence, you may find your head nodding up and down to some rhythm of "I understand," even though you have no words for this, which is beyond any understanding. You may feel your throat open, wanting to say something, or to make some sound. In this land of silence, a sound may well up from deep within.

As the dark silence of your grief comes to know the presence of the great silence beyond all words, you may find a sound spontaneously rising within you, softly flowing from you heart through to your throat, through your body, out your lips, up into the vast heavens. Perhaps something as simple as *La, la, la, lala*, perhaps the sound of a sob.

Softly, over and over again, for a long time, maybe for five minutes or more, moving from soft to loud to louder, back to softer, calling out. You may find grief tears rising from your deepest heart, moving out of you on these sounds that come from your depths and return to silence. Sounds and tears carrying your broken heartedness into the arms of a deep holiness that somehow brings you back into the silenc that holds you and your loved one. Sounds of awe or love or compassion may rise up.

Through the ages, people are called upon to let the sounds of their grief come as they dance upon the ashes. For me, one song arose out of cracks of my broken heart, one song that lives in me still over the many years since my child's death. It is a wordless song, sounding my grief, my love and awe before the ocean of mystery that is both birth and death. Since it is a wordless song, I cannot sing it to you. I can only tell you what the sounds convey to me as my heart sings them:

*Oh, to be a human, to walk each step slowly, with mercy.*

*To give and receive tender comfort.*

*To hears these sounds touch me from the hidden places, how grateful I am.*

The sounds remain as my soul song, and I have shared them with my spiritual director and asked him to sing this wordless song when I am dying and returning to the Great Silence and the Great Love.

## *Guided meditation: Sounding my soul song*

*Sit quietly in meditation in the sacred place you have created for yourself.*

*Close your eyes. Listen and wait.*

*Or come to a meditative awareness during the moments in your day, as you wash the dishes, walk your dog, take an evening stroll.*

*Pause, relax, breathe deeply, come to stillness.*

*Go within and listen to any sounds deep inside you waiting to be heard.*

*Allow the sounds to rise up though your body, through*

*your throat, to your lips, and through your mouth.*

*Let the sounds find their way.*

*Let them have their own life, their own movement.*

*Sighs, whispers, humming, tears, smiles, sobs, a thrumming of breath and heartbeat—the movement of your body.*

*Let these sounds have their time, let them be carried on your breath.*

*Sense the sounds moving within and opening you to your true feelings.*

*Sounds beyond words, sitting deep within your body and spirit.*

*Allow the sounds of loss, missing, deep sadness, love, longing, anger, all moving through you, rising from deep inside to your lips.*

*Know how, as the sounds come through, as you listen to them, you may be touched by feelings you did not even know were in you.*

*Allow your feelings to be carried to you on their sounds.*

*In these sounds, life comes to you.*

*Out of the great silence that surrounds and holds your grief, your songs are being born.*

*Your sounds may carry words as they sing through you.*

*Or, they may be wordless sounds, carrying their own deep meaning, beyond words.*

*As you travel through time on your path of grief, you may find that there is one song that stays with you, becomes your sacred soul song, goes on living in your heart, asks, at unexpected moments, to be sung.*

*Perhaps, over time, you may come to understand the meaning of this wordless song.*

*Perhaps it is a song of praise and gratitude for having loved, for having been given the gift of life and love, for being part of the vast mystery surrounding this life, this death.*

*While journeying in the land of grief, may you find your way to raise yourself into song.*

*May you find your soul voice with which to express your sorrow and your love.*

*May the song leaving your mouth lift your grief into the great mystery of life and death into sacred silence.*

## In your journal

If your song has words, let their sounds write themselves into your journal.

If your song is wordless, sing its sounds over and over.

Sing until you hear what the sounds are saying from your heart.

Listen quietly as the sounds of your song move in your breath, in your body, through your blood stream.

Write what comes out of the sounds onto the page.

Sense the difference of your song when it rises up from your body without words and when your mouth utters words.

Sing back and forth, sing first from words and then from sound.

Pause and listen between each, sense what feelings come to you, draw if you wish.

Listen to the wordless song as you sing.

Sing it for a long time, beyond when you would like to stop singing.

And then be silent. Hear what has been brought to you to feel, to know, to understand of life and death, of loss and grief.

Receive your song as a soul companion on your journey through grief.

Listen as your song rises up, let it sing you.

Sing and listen to what your song stirs in your heart and write.

# 40.

## *I learn the way of compassionate connection*

L OOKING BACK AT THE VAST SEA *of mourning that engulfed me after my daughter died, I am surprised to find memories of people reaching out to connect to me and shore me up. Because I was numb with shock and disorientation, I only dimly sensed the comforts that were brought to me, as one senses being touched when anesthetized.*

*And yet, I do remember and am ever-grateful, even these more than 40 years later, for the touches of comfort that remain imprinted in my memory:*

*Notes I still have, from people I barely knew, offering me their memories of my daughter. A single, white rose in a vase and home-made soup left on my doorstep with a caring note. The friend who phoned every morning that summer, just to say, "I love you. I'm here." A colleague calling to let me know my work life was waiting to cushion me when I was ready to return. My friend Jules, on the first Mother's Day without Leslie, when I couldn't get dressed or even imagine leaving the house, taking my hand, saying, "Come on, you look fine in your bathrobe." We sat at the dock by the bay, talking quietly, or just silent, for a long time, as people came and went.*

There is much more that I do not recall because the pain of grief can wipe out memory and did certainly wipe out much of mine. And yet there remains the indelible knowing that I was not alone. Memories remain of so many reaching out—remembering Leslie; remembering Eric, her father; remembering me.

So many simple acts, nothing extraordinary. Simple human acts touching me, tethering me, not caring that I went out in my bathrobe, so many small acts of connection, so that I knew I was not lost, not swallowed into eternal emptiness, not forgotten, somehow still here. Human light beckoning out to the dark sea of grief, signaling and drawing me to shore.

The heartfelt gestures that touch us on The Path of Grief teach us how connection and survival are woven together, how comfort can touch our numb despair. We learn nothing extraordinary is required.

We witness how the many small, simple acts of kindness move from someone's heart into our sorrow.

We learn that people will sit with us. Even as we are closed off in our grief, they will be there to comfort us. We learn how our actual, physical survival depends on being held in human connection.

We know now there are heart conditions that are called "broken heart syndrome" and come not only from loss of a loved one, but also from the loss of human connection during our grieving. Connection can also come from the loving heart of a beloved pet, keenly feeling our broken heart and not moving from our side.

The comfort of others weaves a circle of loving connection around the mourner. Held in this tender circle, our grief becomes more bearable. Any movement coming that is felt as real will reach the heart of the mourner and may literally save his life.

Sustaining connection is not the privilege of the human family. I was touched to watch on TV a family of elephants slowly circling one of their own as it lay dying—their grief palpable, their tails swaying as one in a somber silent arc. They stayed connected in their circle of love, of loss, and of solace.

Because we know how life-saving connections with others have been in our grief, we learn how sacred our simplest gestures in times of grief can be. And so, we comfort others when it is their time to walk their path of grief. In this way, the wide river of compassion ripples from one heart to another, binding us in a circle of shared consolation and compassion, our hearts moving out to connect with and comfort both those we know and the stranger on our shared path of loss as well.

As I write this, I am sitting on a bench in the park. There is a woman sitting on a bench across from me.

I have never seen her before. I look at her. She is a woman like me, of a certain age. I see the smile lines on her face and the lines of sorrow as well. She is like me, and like you, like each of us, made of tears and smiles. There is no need for us to speak. The woman and I smile at each other, a comforting smile, a connection smile, a smile of knowing between strangers, a smile belonging to our common vulnerable family, alive together on this earth and in need of truly seeing one another, both the broken and the whole of our shared human condition.

# Guided meditation:
## The Blessing Bowl of connection

*Come to your place and time of solitude. Sit quietly.*

*Contemplate the connections in your life that give you and have given you comfort.*

*Let each person from past to present appear before you.*

*Let those who are close family and friends appear.*

*Let those who you barely knew appear.*

*Allow any beloved pets to appear.*

*Breathe, wait, welcome whoever comes to stand before you.*

*Allow yourself to be surprised by who comes.*

*Feel and sense your gratitude, express your thanks to each being who comes with words or a gesture of comfort.*

*Let each know how they now help you or once helped you in your grief and perhaps saved your spirit.*

*Find the place in your body where you can carry these gifts.*

*Allow your hand to rest there. Breathe there. Sense how these gifts of connection live within you.*

*Know how you will always carry them.*

*Feel in your heart how these gifts of connection are now yours to give.*

*Know that your gifts of connecting can be the smallest of gestures.*

*Only that they come from your compassionate heart*

*Sense your heart as a Blessing Bowl, holding the gifts of connection that came to you as you journeyed through the land of grief.*

*Know how now the Blessing Bowl of you heart can bless others with simple acts of kindness in their time of grief.*

*Let yourself know also that you can extend your Blessing*

*Bowl to those you do not know personally, to those who may live far away in need of consolation.*

*You can do this by breathing in, receiving their grief, as a dark color, and breathing out to them a healing light of solace.*

*And, too, let yourself be aware of our Mother Earth and her need to have her suffering known in the hearts of humans, her need to be connected with in healing ways of reverence. Breathe in the dark pain of Mother Earth and breathe a beautiful, healing light back to her.*

## *In your journal*

Open your journal. See those who appeared before you in your meditation.

Let yourself feel and know how essential their presence to you was and still is.

Feel your gratitude.

Write to each of them, letting them know how you hold them in your heart.

Thank them for being in your life.

You may wish to write a letter to some or to all of these people who connected to you in your time of grief to tell them how exactly they provided the sustenance of human connection for you.

They may not know that they touched you in your grief, recently or long ago.

On this journey, there is no such thing as time, only the timeless threads of connection woven by the heart.

You may wish to draw a heart, your heart upon the journal page, and to write in it the names of all those who are woven in your heart as dots of light where comfort has touched.

# 41.

## *I let new loved ones gradually enter my life*

WHILE MOURNING THE LOSS OF YOUR LOVED ONE and the loss of your life as it had been, it may be hard to imagine forming new, meaningful relationships with others. People you see outside your circle of old friends may seem foreign, for they have no connection to the one we grieve. No one knows about your life back home in your old country. Your old country is invisible to others, who do not know the landscape of your former life.

But, it is possible that people who were once only acquaintances or even strangers may become new friends. As you take tentative steps into the stream of life again, you may begin to build a bridge to new relationships and experiences. But you need to be cautious. If you jump too quickly into a busy life with new relationships and activities, you may abandon the time and space you need to be with your loss.

On the other hand, if you stay locked in the old country, close yourself off from creating new and meaningful relationships, you will be dogged by loneliness and isolation for a long time, perhaps for the rest of your life.

*After his wife died, Michael went to sleep each night tenderly touching the pillow on her side of the bed. In this way, he said goodnight to her. Each morning, he would pat her pillow and straighten any wrinkles. For two years, he carried out his ritual of keeping his wife beside him, so in dread was he to face the emptiness of his loss.*

*One part of him recognized his wife was gone. Another part of him denied her death.*

*Michael did not meet new friends or invite anyone to his home, lest the past be disturbed, like some wrinkle on his wife's pillow.*

*One day, Michael arrived at my office carrying his wife's pillow in his arms.*

*He held it close to him and wept as he talked to her: My love, I cannot keep holding on to you. I want to but if I am to live, I must let go. I need to find a way to live without you." He looked up at me and asked me to help him. I promised that we would do our best.*

Michael's tight hold on his past highlights the struggle many of us have accepting our losses and opening to new beginnings. Michael kept his wife's pillow beside him in bed. Now, upon awaking, he began to tell her aloud of his plans for the day. In this way, he felt his connection with his wife as he began to find his way forward. While contemplating new beginnings, you may enter a struggle that takes time and cannot be forced. This movement toward going forward has its own organic rhythm. As new friendships and courtships organically begin to form, we may find ourselves amazed that our hearts are able to gradually open and even love again.

Somehow, we do love again, and yet it is a different love than the one we had known. We are surprised by how new love does not take the place of old love, as we had feared. We are surprised by how many different kinds of love we are capable of. We come to see that no love takes the place of any other. We come to realize the diamond of our heart has many facets of loving, able to know the uniqueness of each person we love. We come to sense our capacity to love as ever-expanding and deepening. The love we have known with the one who has died has become our teacher in learning that love itself is all that matters.

Since the loss of my daughter, the look of love on her sleepy face as she awakened from her nap guides my eyes to share tenderness with others, friends and strangers, alike. In such moments of seeing the other, even if fleeting, I sense our shared humanity, witnessing one another on our common human journey, of being human beings together in this life. In this way, the love I have for my daughter lives on.

As I grow older, my love for my daughter goes on and on in ever-widening circles. This is what love does. This is what loss does. Our journey of love and loss teaches us how vulnerable and how precious all of life is. Loss and love teach us to give our heart to the living moment, to the face and heart of the one right in front of us, because otherwise this moment will pass like a cloud and our chance to share love will vanish.

Sometimes, in the beginning moments of a new relationship, you may find yourself stepping back, feeling that familiar ache of loss, feel tears well up. You may wonder how you can laugh with these people, these strangers, in this foreign country. You may ask, "Who am I? This refugee from the country of grief, how shall I go on?

We go on, come to know we do not betray our past, nor leave our loved one behind, nor ever forget.

Rather, as we go on, we continue the love, hear their laughter in our own, recognize their presence in our gestures, their values in our deeds. We are carrying the best of our love for them and their love for us into the future. We are keeping our love alive and enriching our new relationships with that love. We are coming to understand how we can touch and be touched by new lives in our new country, while still missing and sometimes aching for our old life. This is how we come to live in the full portion of both our grief and our love.

## Guided meditation: Gestures of new beginnings

*Sit quietly and ponder the opening to new people and new relationships in your life:*

*Friends, acquaintances, neighbors, co-workers, and classmates.*

*Is there someone you want to get to know better? Someone you might like as a friend?*

*Can you envision reaching out to connect, inviting them over, accepting an invitation?*

*See yourself making this gesture of reaching out toward a new connection.*

*Feel the movement of reaching out in your body.*

*Know how large a gesture it is to move into new life, to reach out, to open yourself to go on.*

*Ask if this is the right time for you to move out to take steps into a new country.*

*If so, let your desire open in your meditation, not forcing, allowing your true rhythm.*

*You may say aloud from your heart's desire: "I will let new people into my life.*

*I will open the door of my heart and move out into the world.*

*At the same time, I will cherish and honor my life with my loved one.*

*I will share the love we have known together with new people.*

*I understand our love will never die, the best of us will sustain me, will radiate from the center of my being.*

*The love we shared that lives in me will sustain others: family, friends, acquaintances, and strangers I may encounter along the way.*

*My dear one who has died, as I go on, you go on as well as a part of my essence.*

*Please know I will always honor and show gratitude for our relationship, our love, and for life itself."*

*And if the time for reaching toward new life in this way is not right for you, may the possibility of desire sit in you like a hidden seed, growing somewhere deep in your being.*

*May you trust that its time for ripening will eventually come.*

## *In your journal*

As you sit in your place of solitude or take a quiet walk, have your journal with you.

Sit with the question: Is there anyone I would like to get to know? Take a walk with? Share a dinner with? Go to a concert with? Have an intimate time of conversation with?

Sit and feel this movement of desire in your body. Where does it sit? Let the energy of your desire move. Sit quietly, feel the movement of aliveness. Let it speak on to your journal page.

Then, sit quietly again. See what arises in your body now. Is there a place in your body that tightens with a "No" to your desire? Feel the energy and where the "No" sits in your body. Let this "No" to your desire write itself onto a facing journal page.

Try not to label either feeling good or bad, negative or positive. Just give them each your presence.

Listening as you place a hand on each voice, feeling each movement of energy.

Let your two feelings speak to one another. Write the dialogue. Write for 15 minutes. If you want to stop, keep writing for a while longer. Often, lifting our pen off the page is a way of not being with an uncomfortable feeling.

After you have written in your journal, take the time to be open, to not having a clear sense of how to proceed.

Place one hand over your desire to go forward and the other hand upon your "No" to that desire. Take your time. Go back and forth from one hand to the other. Listen. Sense.

Has anything shifted? Listen. If clarity does not come, see if there is a third place in your body that holds some feeling. Place your hands there. Listen. Hear. Write.

May you be patient with this process, understanding the time it takes to step from the land of loss and love onto the bridge of new beginnings.

# 42.

## *I live the essence of my loved one*

OUR PHYSICAL SENSES CANNOT RETAIN and embrace forever the voice, the facial expressions, or the touch of a loved one who has disappeared. No matter how we try to hold on, our sense impressions weaken and gradually fade when one who was a part of our life is no longer physically with us. Their disappearance leaves empty, bewildered spaces, leaves us in a wilderness of lost sense memory.

I remember how, several months after my daughter died, her little friend Sari came close up to me and, wide-eyed, said in a soft, bewildered voice: "I can't hear Leslie's voice anymore."

I know this sense of bewilderment when faced with the mysterious way our five senses refuse to hold fast to our most precious memories. We want to hold on as long as we can to the smile, to the tilt of her head, to the bounce in his step, the sound of her voice. But, in time, our memories become distant, like some lovely music that has slowly grown faint until we can barely hear it. Our visual memories become like faded photographs. Like Sari, we feel bewildered at how our loved one has vacated our seeing, our hearing, our touch.

But then, from out of nowhere, a sense memory comes back, like an echo. The turn of our loved one's head, the way she brushed away a wisp of hair, the way his eyes closed while he listened to music.

Suddenly our sense memory reawakens, stays for a vivid moment, and then fades once again.

I will always miss the pride with which Leslie sat so tall on her daddy's shoulders. The way Nina looked out at the world with bright, wide Christmas-light eyes. The quiet tender eyes of my father. The deep, belly laugh of my mother. At times, unexpectedly, I see and hear again, feel them right here, unexpectedly, in a vivid memory lit up and full of grace.

Just yesterday, as I was taking a walk, for a flicker of a moment, I saw my daughter running toward me across the field, her arms out-stretched. Just the way she used to. I could almost hear her calling, "Mommy, I'm coming." A moment of illuminated memory returns and is just as suddenly gone.

These flashes of illuminated memory are nurtured by love. As our sense memory fades, something else grows strong in its place. Some-thing indelible remains behind in the vessel of our hearts, something that survives our frail senses to hold the essence of those we love. Along The Path of Grief, seeds of their essential being take root deep in our being. It may be true that our senses are weak, but our love remains strong, nourishing and watering the essence of our loved one, implant-ing in our hearts as seeds of love. The essence of our loved one stays with us, entwines and blossoms with our essence, and is slowly woven into our being as a part of us. In this way, our relationship goes on in an abiding embrace of love.

*Sally's "Hello" was always reserved and shy. After her husband died, Sally found herself saying, "Hi!" with an unaccustomed gusto as she passed someone she knew on the street or as she made friendly eye contact with a stranger.*

*This "Hi!" is a full-bodied greeting she has polished with a warm smile. It is a new kind of hello for Sally: It is her husband's hello, the one she used to admire so much for its warmth. Now, her husband's hello lives as it sounds through the aliveness of Sally's hello.*

*Sally is not copying her husband's way of saying hello. This new hello is not a simple imitation. Her husband's hello has become woven into the fabric of Sally's being. Her beloved husband is always with her, a part of her, living in her hello. Yes, Sally will forever miss her husband's living presence. She will go on living with the paradox of his not being there and then suddenly sense him as a warm presence entwined with and expressed through her being.*

It is true that with the loss of our loved one, we suffer not only the loss of their physical being but also the loss of the memories of their everyday presence in our lives. We are bereft of their physical presence, the dimming of our sense memories, of our shared life with them. And yet, with time, we find ourselves surprised by how our loved one's way of being goes on with us as a part of our own being.

The essence of the other seems to shine forth into our living, in our laughter, in our smile, in the way we see with our eyes and heart, in our hellos and goodbyes, in all that we treasure.

## Guided meditation: Carrying my loved one on

*Choose your time to sit quietly in your place of solitude.*

*Come to quiet breathing, in and out, waiting in the pause for the next breath.*

*Sit with the question: What of your loved one lives in our life and heart and memory?*

*Take your time.*

*Sense and feel what of your loved one's nature is now a part of who you are.*

*Look into your heart and find there the essence of this person you love.*

*What of his values? Her capacity to feel another's pain? His joy of life?*

*Her love of quiet of music or art? His generosity to both family and stranger?*

*What of her gestures? The way he stopped to pet a dog? The way he began or ended a meal? The way she lingered weeding the garden?*

*What of this beloved goes on being a part of you, the ways in which you cherish and continue a loved one's life as part of your own?*

*As you sit, aware of the qualities and values of your loved one and sense them living on in you, take the time to contemplate these aspects of your shared being.*

*What is it like for you, what does it mean to you, to carry on these qualities?*

*What do they hold for you? What do they say about living a good life?*

*Take the time to listen to how your body feels, to carry your loved one as part of your embodied self.*

*Body to body. Soul to soul.*

*Take some time to be aware of your gratitude for the ways in which your loved is carried forth by you.*

## *In your journal*

Write in your journal those qualities of your loved one now living through you.

As you name those qualities, pause at each one.

Take your time. Write what each quality means to you.

Take time to write of your commitment to keep alive in your living those qualities of your loved one most precious to you.

Feel and write of the deep and sacred space within where the essential being of your loved one is nurturing the ways you are living your life.

Sense how remembering and honoring his or her essential life keeps the two of you close, your life and theirs becoming a part of the turning of the wheel of all life.

Gather your feelings and then write.

# 43.

## *I look at life with new amazement*

SOMETIMES, IN THE MIDST OF OUR GRIEF, we are suddenly moved by a grace at the heart of things. We feel a new sense of reverence for all of life, a heightened appreciation for everything around us. We look at a sunset, look into a face, watch the falling rain and feel a deep sigh within; it is the sound of our own growing amazement at the myriad ways in which sacredness of life shines through. Our mind and heart are seeing life as if for the first time. We are like a young child, in wonder, pointing a finger toward a newborn kitten and crying out, "Oh! Look!"

With "beginner's mind," shaped by our encounter with death and grief, we find ourselves seeing the precious movement of life in all that is. We wonder at the deep mystery of how we could possibly open after being frozen in sorrow. But we know we have been expanded beyond our limitations and the limits of time and space to behold the very mystery of life, the presence of the infinite indwelling in our moments. In our amazement, we see the force of creation everywhere, and especially within the ordinary moments of our daily life.

It is a wonder how we now find something to cherish in the smallest of things. We don't need to visit the Grand Canyon to be awed. We can slowly drink a cold glass of water, sit under a leafy or bare tree, play with a child, sit beside an elder, or watch our dog stop to sniff the grass. We find a quiet radiance shining through the day's moments. We find ourselves no longer interested in possessing the moments, evaluating the circumstances, or analyzing our experiences: It is enough to look, to appreciate, to touch what we encounter, and to be touched in return. Somehow, along the journey of our grief, life becomes simplified. As we return to life, we do not need "big" experiences in order to appreciate the wonders of life. Nor do we need any longer to live up to some big expectation of who we are supposed to be. We are simply "here," called forth by life, responding to life, saying, "I am here. I am here to meet you, life," as if we hear life calling to us, "Where are you? Come!"

In the journey of our grieving, we have somehow gained the knowledge of how small we are in the face of death and in the brilliance of the light of life. It is precisely because we have come to know how small we are and how fleeting our life is that we feel amazement at the infinite wonder of all life, including our own. Because we have squinted through the darkness of grief, we can see the radiance that shines in the living.

It is something I will never understand, how out of the darkness of grief, a divine light comes to let me know I, too, am this divine light of the universe that is in all things. Somehow, out of the darkest darkness, I see life filled with light. I see my life, your life, as light, and know each life is filled with light. I know this light is always here with me, even when I fall back into the deepest darkness. We are each made of both darkness and light, like the darkness at the center of the candle flame that is surrounded by light.

Along the long journey of love and loss, grief has taught me to take this light and wrap it around my darkness. I know now that when I fall into darkness, if I wait with faith, light waits for me to journey where I must and then returns to touch me.

Grief has taught me that being in the darkness also has its time. Like the moon waxing and waning, we move through the dark and the light. In the dark, I must wait. Grief has taught me light is here even when I cannot see it. Out of grief, in the incubating darkness, faith is formed, a coming to know that in the dark little dots of holy light are forming.

Grief is a teacher, guiding us to offer ourselves to this source of light, when we go to sleep, when we wake up, as we walk through our day. Grief teaches us to offer ourselves and lift all things to this light of life with gratitude. This is the spiritual practice that grief the teacher brings to us. This is the way in which our grief matures into a sense of grace for all of life.

I don't know why I wasn't aware of this light before I knew grief. I just wasn't. Maybe I took life for granted, didn't lift my eyes to see how golden and short-lived it all is. I share my experience with you who may be sitting on the dark, barren ground of your grief in the hope you may sense a small glimmer of light somewhere along the path on your journey.

If you cannot yet find that glimmer, may there be those who love you, as there were for me, carrying the light for you until you can once again carry it for yourself.

## Guided meditation: Life going on

*Set aside brief times during your day to pause in whatever you are doing.*

*Breathe, look at life all around you.*

*Look around you with a beginner's mind to see one thing living fresh.*

*Be with what your eyes come upon, linger, slow down, pause, see, listen to whatever may call you attention.*

*Choose to look, gaze upon, contemplate what is before you: the apple you are holding, the taste of it, the tree just outside your window, the sky dappled with clouds.*

*See, as if for the first time.*

*Listen, as if for the first time*

*Taste, as if for the first time.*

*Let your eyes linger, take your time, stop and notice.*

*Let yourself be touched as you take in, with your eyes and heart, young lovers strolling, hands entwined.*

*A stranger standing next to you on the street corner who surely also knows of loss and love.*

*A mother tenderly holding her child's hand.*

*The man in a wheelchair enjoying his ice cream cone.*

*Whatever you see, linger, look.*

*Let what you see come alive for you.*

*Let it touch your aliveness.*

*Let it touch your numbness.*

*For a single moment, be stirred by the wonder of life, even if, just now, you do not feel a part of it.*

*Your grief may cause you to see life from a distance, far from any light.*

*Even so, you may be moved to tears to see the simple moments of life while you are grieving.*

*Grief itself may be opening your heart to the sacred life of all living things.*

*Let the tears come, for they too are a part of being alive.*

*Before you wipe them away, let them come down your face.*

*Be touched by your tears, feel your tears holding life.*

*Grief for your loss and gratitude for the precious goodness of life.*

*Let them sit side by side. Allow them; breathe in and breathe out.*

*Rest in the pause.*

*Allow yourself to be a full human being, living with all that is the truth of your reality.*

*Precious heart-touching moments of living, sad heart touching loss and leavings.*

*Alongside the sadness of your heart, may you find yourself feeling moved, quickened by the grace and grandeur of life moving in the smallest of things: in your tears and smiles, in your going on, in your light and darkness.*

## *In your journal*

During your day, take time, as if a bell is being rung, calling you to stop what you are doing.

Breathe, come to quiet.

Look in front of you, behind you, to each side of you.

Pause where you are touched by something by someone. Look. See. Listen.

Take a few minutes, let your eyes, and heart, and breathing linger.

Write in your journal. See what it's like not to write in sentences.

Let your seeing write what your eyes touch.

Let your hearing write what feelings the sounds echo in you.

Leaf falling slowly from tree, letting go.

In lamp light, moth glowing, amazing, beauty, so small.

Restaurant dinner across the way, old man, head dropped, her hand on his, still young lovers.

Write simply, simple words, of what you see, hear, all that touches you with life.

# 44.

## *I live open to the unknown*

I SIT, WRITING AT A DESK IN NEW MEXICO, in a house on a mesa. I am here alone. Through the wall of windows before me, I see a vast sky filled with grey clouds drifting in a bright blue sky. Maybe it will rain. Maybe it won't. The only sound I hear is silence. Then a bird flutters its wings. Then all is silence again. Then distant thunder. Then the thunder stops. Will the rain come? Maybe. Eventually. When? I do not know.

Will death come? Yes. Like thunder, lightning, and rain, like the fluttering of wings, like a quiet breath, death will come. But I don't know when. All things come and go. The clouds. The birds. The rain. The thunder. Breathing in. Breathing out. Life itself. We live in the space between birth and death. The question is when will life cross over into death? We don't know, and yet we live like the answer is never; we live as if life will go on forever, as if there is no unknowing woven into the heart of our existence.

In the Buddhist tradition, there is a practice of placing a human skull at the doorway of one's home, a reminder as we go out into the world and return home that the threshold of coming and going, of life and death, waits to be crossed. In the Jewish tradition, the white coat worn by a man at his wedding is the same coat he will be buried in. The prayer shawl he is given at age 13 to signify his passage out of boyhood into manhood is the same shawl he will wear when he makes his passage from life to death. In the Native American tradition, there are tribes whose members lie alive in the graves that will be theirs and practice their death. These rituals sharpen our awareness that death is a reality, ever-present in the midst of our lives.

If we live without these ritual reminders, when death does come, we will feel a sense of shock, a shattering of our illusion that the next step in front of us is solid. We will be unprepared for what death demands of us. We need such rituals to open our awareness, to remind us that life really is impermanent and our illusions of anything other ultimately do not sustain us. Our religious, spiritual, and cultural rituals help us practice gazing into the bright sun of the reality of death without putting on sunglasses to obscure the light.

When death comes, as we enter the landscape of our grief, we realize profoundly how we live in a world of utter unknowing and impermanence.

*"You know, Mommy, I'm going very far away. I'm going where it never rains, and it never snows. And, you can't come with me. Mommy."*

I thought Leslie was playing a game with me. But now I believe she was preparing me to come face-to-face with the unknown, with the glaring light of her impending death. I understand now, so many years later, that, for my daughter, the veil between this world and the invisible world beyond was not yet fully drawn. That she would suddenly become ill and die before her mother and father, this was unknowable and unthinkable. Why she wanted to wear only yellow, the color of her golden hair and of the sun, in those weeks before she died was unknown. Why a yellow butterfly rested on the railing of the terrace outside her hospital room the moment she parted from the cocoon of her body was unknown.

The death of my daughter helped me understand in my marrow that we live in a vast ocean of the unknown and unknowable—as endless, vast blue sky above me as I write. We are adrift in mystery, in the unfathomable, and our sense of security and invulnerability are illusions that shatter with the loss of a loved one. On the journey of our grief, we come to live with a sense of holy insecurity, with a deep humility, face-to-face with the presence of death in our lives.

When death comes, it erases our false sense of security, obliterates our certainties, and changes our view that we live on solid ground. Thrown onto The Path of Grief and into the land of loss, we come to know, profoundly, that we do not know: We come face-to-face with the precariousness at the heart of our lives. We learn we are mortal; we learn we are all mortal; and we understand fully that we do not know when death will come for us. We learn how vulnerable and in need of one another's caring we all really are.

From death, out of our loss, into our grief comes a knowing that what we think of as solid in our lives can be washed away in an instant, like sand castles at the edge of the sea. This knowing instills in us the wish to take care of even the smallest things of life, seeing how fleeting and fragile and sacred we are to flower for our brief time. This intimate knowing of the impermanence of all that lives opens our hearts to the mystery of life and death, to how all things come and go, are born, receive the blessing of life, and then die.

When death comes, we watch powerless, in awe, as our loved one begins their journey into the unknown. When death comes, profound sadness and poignancy become a part of our lives, along with a deep sense of gratitude and joy for all life. We become deeply caring midwives for one another in the mysterious passage into this life and from this life into death.

# *Guided meditation: I behold the mystery*

*In the quiet of your being, know how we are each a mystery.*

*Know how we each come from and return to mystery.*

*Sense the unknown and the unknowable woven into the fabric of your life, into all of life.*

*Look long and deeply into the faces of your family and friends, one face at a time.*

*See the mystery of each one, sense the mystery of yourself.*

*From where did each of you come? To where shall each of you go?*

*To what or whom do your lives belong?*

*As well as you think you know them, or yourself, contemplate how we are all a part of the vast mystery of life.*

*See each of you as truly unknowable, fragile, and mysterious beings.*

*Be aware as you look at yourself, at each person, including strangers on the street, how in the vast unfolding time of this universe, our time on this earth is as fleeting as a blink of the eye.*

*Breathe in. Breathe out.*

*Sense how, built into your very breath, is the coming and going of all things.*

*Breathe in. Breathe out.*

*As you breathe, let yourself feel the awe of the mystery of both breath and being.*

*Know how they are one.*

*Contemplate your own mystery:*

*How well do you think you know yourself? What will happen to you next?*

*How long do you have in this life? Why are you here?*

*To whom or what does your life belong?*

*To whom or what does your very breath belong?*

*To whom or what does your time belong?*

*As you look around, really see the people passing by, notice and be aware: That baby will soon grow old; that woman is close to death; your partner, your friend, may or may not exist next year; you will vanish as well, not knowing when or to where.*

*May your heart in the brokenness of grief come to hold all life in tender embrace.*

## *In your journal*

Sit with all you feel as you contemplate this reflection.

How is it for you to sit with the mystery and impermanence of all that is?

Of your loved ones and yourself?

Slowly, take time to write what comes up in your feelings and thoughts as you reflect on being a mystery to your own self. Write what comes up for you.

Is this true to your experience of yourself? Of those close to you?

What is your sense of this mystery? Write what comes up for you.

Write about what happens for you when you contemplate your own impermanence and that of those close to you.

Mindful of the fleetingness of all life, do your eyes and heart see differently in any way? Write.

Are you perhaps stirred to care more deeply, more tenderly, for the people in your life, for the stranger you hold the door for, because you see and know how fragile, how fleeting and vulnerable we all are?

Write.

# 45.

## *I live with the reverence of acceptance*

ONCE I HEARD A STORY ABOUT A MAN who placed a folded piece of paper into each of his pants pockets every morning. On one he wrote, "*I am made of dust and I will return to dust.*" On the other he wrote, "*Today, the world was created just for me.*" Carrying this paradox in his awareness every day—that he is everything, and the world needs him and counts on him, and that he is dust and will return to dust; he is impermanent. In this way, the man went about his life.

When I imagine this man, I see him living with a keen awareness of his death and with the same keen awareness of his life. Although loss has given him the certainty that he will die, he also knows he was born just so he could live the life only he was put here on this earth to live.

Acceptance doesn't mean defeat or bitter resignation to a fate we cannot change. True acceptance means we know how precarious life is but understand, in sacred silence, the mystery of things greater than ourselves. We accept we are finite and we accept we are infinite, and we allow our life to flow with infinite possibility. We accept both of these profound messages and we carry them in our pockets, every day, balancing the visible and the invisible, heaven and earth, life and death in our everyday encounters.

On The Path of Grief, as you learn to live with your loss, you may find your simplest encounters with life carrying a sense of the holy: a quiet meal, a walk with a friend, the sounds of music, the fading light of dusk, the first star in the heavens, the coming light of dawn. Each unfolding a wonder to behold.

But then, as time goes on, we forget, the veil falls, and once again we take life for granted—we take the air we breathe for granted, we take our loved ones for granted. We cannot help forgetting: We have many concerns and our hearts and senses are dulled by all of our doing, by forgetting to come home to the center of our being, to the being of life's living moments.

But then, when our remembrance of death does return, it shakes our heart awake; we touch the papers in our pockets; and the paradox of existence startles us once again.

Recently, I was standing in line at the local café, taking a break from work to treat myself to a cappuccino. The young woman at the espresso machine was new on the job and she was very slow. I took my place at the back of a long line and soon lost my patience and found myself frowning at the struggling barista. Then, in a moment, I imagined others in front of me frowning at her as well, and I wondered how she must feel to see a long line of disgruntled faces staring at her.

It was then that I reached into my pockets to touch the pieces of paper I'd placed there that morning, and I remembered: I am dust. You are dust. We are each dust. And, the world was created for me, for you, for each of us. In that moment, as I looked at the young woman, I whispered the Buddhist prayer of loving kindness:

*May you be happy. May you be well. May you know ease in your life.*

And I added: *May you see in our faces patience and gratitude for serving us.*

Each day after that, I looked forward to coming to the café, so I could practice the awareness tucked into my two pockets and turn impatience into a loving kindness that honored the new barista's precious life.

## Guided meditation: I am dust, for me the world was made

*Write on one piece of paper:* I am made of dust and will return to dust.

*On another piece of paper, write:* Today, the world was created just for me.

*Put these papers in each of your pockets or in your purse.*

*Carry them with you through the day.*

*Remember to touch them at moments as you go through your day.*

*Meditate on them, reflect on their meaning for your life.*

*Touch them whenever you think of them.*

*Notice what you are feeling as you touch each paper.*

*Meditate on what it means to be aware of your death and aware of your singular life at the same time.*

*Be aware of sending the kindness of your face to those you encounter along the way.*

*To those you know, to a stranger you may sit near, to those dear to you, to someone you have trouble with, to yourself.*

*To each one who will become dust, to each one born, to offer something of his or her life to life.*

*For the sake of sacred life, breathing, being mindful.*

*Breathing your stress into gratitude, your impatience into blessing, breathing tenderness toward your own self.*

*Be aware of the spirit of your loved one, whose body has returned to dust, smiling upon you with great love, blessing you.*

*May you be happy. May you be well. May you know peace and joy.*

*May you hold the two pieces of paper.*

*May you know you are dust.*

*May you know life depends upon you.*

*May you hold the two pieces of paper in your pockets as you reach out to the world, as your heart beholds precious life in its fleeting and infinite beauty.*

## *In your journal*

On one side of your journal, write: "I am dust and will return to dust."

Write all that comes up for you as you bring awareness to this truth.

Be aware of your feelings.

Be aware of where they arise in your body.

Take your time, feel, and sense what comes.

On the facing page write: "Today, the world was created for me."

Under these words, write all that comes into your awareness.

Write your feelings, your body sense.

Take your time.

# 46.

## *My life becomes simpler*

BEFORE HIS WIFE'S DEATH, LEO'S LIFE *had been consumed with business appointments and family obligations. He and his wife seldom ate dinner or spent relaxed weekends together. After his wife's death, Leo was hit hard by grief. The wind went out of his sails. He was no longer able to go at the pace he had kept up his entire adult life. The loss of his wife brought him to a standstill, lost at sea.*

*Leo took a sabbatical from work. He sat at home, spending hours by himself. One day, he noticed the curtain over the open living room window moving ever so slightly in the breeze. He watched the sunlight play over the leaves of the plant sitting on the window sill. He began noticing other things, too, simple things he'd never noticed before, and they began to touch him, as if to say, "There is life, there is tender life all around you, along with the ache of the loss of your wife's life." He felt more present to his surroundings and told me that this was the first time in his life he had ever been aware of and moved by small things.*

*In these moments of new awareness, Leo felt the presence of his wife: "I think she has guided me home." As he said this, Leo placed his hand over his heart and wept. As Leo came back to life, he felt his wife's presence all around him, as if the new, deep appreciation of life he was experiencing as he slowed down was her gift to him.*

*As Leo discovered a quiet presence with the simple things of life, he took in the comfort of setting the table and eating a meal he had prepared for himself. As he lit a candle, one evening, he told me he recalled how when his wife had lit the candles, he was usually thinking of something left over from his work day instead of sharing this ritual of gratitude for being together at the end of the day. Now, Leo sits quietly for a moment looking at the glow of the candlelight before eating. He eats slowly, savors the flavors as if for the first time. He invites friends over to a quiet Friday evening of dinner and conversation. He says he feels his wife is guiding him now in how to go on living a slower life of appreciation of small things. He feels grateful for her presence and sad that he had taken the sacred moments for granted when she was alive.*

I hear from friends and clients that somehow their lives became simplified after having lost someone they love. That is also my experience: Who would have ever thought that out of the traumatic loss of my child, the grief agony to my body and soul would somehow slowly turn toward a passion for the light of life that shines through the simplest things? It is my experience that the essence of my daughter's being, her light, shines through the light of life and as well through my heart and my eyes as I pause throughout my day to behold the wonder of the shimmering blades of grass growing by the wayside.

Over and over again, in my therapy practice, sitting with bereaved people, I hear how the craving for accomplishment and recognition subsides as we begin to live more by a sense of being than doing. We find refuge in the moments that open and shine right before us: We find ourselves living more in the moment. Our senses become quickened, alerted by the smallest signs of priceless life: the sound of a bird hidden somewhere high in a tree, a tear on someone's cheek, the scent of freshly baked bread, laughter across the room, a rose bud opening into flower. Simple things. The shining forth of life.

At my 50th birthday party, a friend asked me, "What do you wish for the next 50 years?" I was surprised to hear myself say, "I want to become simpler and simpler. . .and simpler. . . until. . ."

As I look back from this vantage point of many years later, I see how those unexpected words spoken from my heart struck a bell that has reverberated through my life ever since. That bell called me to abide in simplicity, and now it calls me back when I have gone too far afield and am doing too much instead of living from the simple core of my being.

Out of our grief journey, our being and doing come more into balance. The words "healing" and "wholeness" and "holy" derive from the same root, and they ring the bell that calls us to be with the light as it falls on the leaf of the plant, to be with the glistening of a freshly cut pear. To be present in the moment with what is right before us.

Death, as it takes away dear life, brings a paradox: being face-to-face with death brings us face-to-face with life. Coming to intimacy with death and life brings us face-to-face with all that sits so simply in the midst of our lives, calling to be honored and tended. All that must not be taken for granted.

May death beckon you to live, to slow down, to be stirred by wonder and steeped in gratitude for the 10,000 things of this life.

## Guided meditation: Begin with a fruit

*Begin with a fruit: an orange, a grapefruit, an apple.*

*Sit with it.*

*Hold it in your hands.*

*Notice the color. Feel the texture.*

*Take in the scent.*

*Sit and contemplate the miracle of this simple fruit.*

*Peel the fruit.*

*Or cut it into pieces, slowly, deliberately, touching, feeling, smelling its aliveness*

*As you eat, taste every bite.*

*Chew slowly, very slowly.*

*Savor the wholeness, the holiness, the simple wonder of this fruit.*

*Picture where it grew, how it grew from a seed, deep in the soil.*

*Contemplate the sheer wonder of the growing of this fruit.*

*Contemplate the ripening, the people who tended and brought this fruit to you.*

*Be thankful for each miracle that placed this fruit upon your table.*

*Know how you and this fruit are alike: filled with the wonder of being a part of all creation.*

*Come to your breathing as you sense your gratitude and awe for the seemingly simple and sacred things of your life*

## In your journal

During your day, stop to pause each time you feel touched by some small thing, perhaps the fruit you are holding and eating.

At the end of your day, as you sit in your quiet place to revisit your day, write about the things and people who called you to stop and take notice. You may draw these things as well capturing something of the quality that touched you.

# 47.

## *The doors of my grief open and close*

SOMEONE RECENTLY SENT ME a postcard of a series of doors, one behind the other. Each door became smaller and smaller as it receded into a vanishing point in the far distance. I wondered if the doors continued beyond the point where I could see them.

As I looked at these doors, I imagined them to be the doors of grief, seen at a greater and greater distance, but always there, always ready to open, close, and open again.

*Isaac is in a restaurant with his wife. An older man and a younger man walk in together and are seated at the next table. There seems to be a special bond between them. As Isaac watches them, an old grief opens; it is the ache of missing his grandfather. Isaac continues eating and chatting with his wife. When the two men get up to leave, he says goodnight to them, as if he knows them well.*

There are echoes of loss and love deep within and all around us. No matter how long it has been since our loved one died, no matter two months, two years, 20 years, and more, sudden, unexpected moments trigger memories and bring tears to our eyes: the silent beauty of falling snow, an elderly couple blessed to grow old together, a strain of familiar music, the laughter of a child. The doors at the beginning of our grief journey will open a gaping entryway into our pain of loss when we encounter such moments of love and beauty.

However, as time passes, seeing a couple holding hands, a grandfather and grandson lingering over coffee, or bouquets of daffodils in a flower stall may feel more like a familiar tap on a distant door; we may feel a wistful, tender love tinged with sadness. Tears may come. Sometimes, they will be tears of heartbreak. More often, they will be the tears of "I know this feeling, I have been there, I remember that deep, precious part of my life I miss so dearly."

As time goes by and the doors of grief become more distant, we find how our tears and smiles have drawn a map upon our face and upon our soul of our love and our loss and of our spiritual journey through grief.

*I am at a supermarket, rushing to get my shopping done. Company is coming for dinner. I'm in a good mood, humming as I go up and down the aisles. As I turn a corner, suddenly, I see a mother ahead of me. She is holding the hand of a little girl with blonde curls. I stop humming. From the back, she looks just like my little girl, Leslie, who died 40 years ago, yesterday.*

*I walk haltingly behind them. A wave of sudden sorrow washes over me. It lasts for a long moment, as the past floods and then unwinds from this present moment.*

*Finally, I look at them and smile, seeing how lovely they are together: how blessed they are, how blessed I was. It is my smile seeing them. It is Leslie's smile as well.*

*The door of my grief opens and closes.*

I believe that even though we move on; renew our lives; and may be blessed with new marriages, children, family and friends, the doors of grief are still there, still opening and closing, only becoming more and more distant, like the doors in the photograph.

I once told a friend that there is a wound in those who mourn that never entirely closes. She said, "But then the wound cannot have been healed. Once a wound is healed, it doesn't open again." I recall being stunned by what she said. It sounded so logical and reasonable that it should have been true and is mostly true of our physical wounds.

But I do not believe it to be true of the wounds of our grief, that, once closed, they remain closed, no longer opening. Like the doors on the postcard our grief grows more faint with distance.

As we survive the journey through our grief, we go on living. We both renew our lives, and the doors of our loss go on opening and closing, opening and closing, time and time again, for the remainder of our lives—our loss and our love forever entwined with one another.

## Guided meditation: Going through the door of loss

*Sit in the quiet of meditation. Follow your breathing in and out.*

*Let your exhalation become long; let your exhalation lead you to a door.*

*See yourself standing in front of the door. See what it is made of.*

*See what the doorknob is made of.*

*See that written on the door is the single word, "Loss."*

*Be in touch with the feelings that arise as you stand in front of the door.*

*Contemplate the word 'Loss' written on the door.*

*If your loss is fresh, know how you are standing in pain at the new door of your grief.*

*Allow the tears that may come as you stand there.*

*If your loss has taken place some time ago, feel how you are standing in front of a more distant door.*

*Allow your feelings to come. Be with whatever arises.*

*Now, place your hand on the door open the door.*

*Enter the place of your loss.*

*What space opens to you: A room? A garden? A cemetery?*

*Look all around to see where you are. What or who do you find there?*

*What or who waits there for you? Take your time. Allow all that wants to happen.*

*Now, breathe in, exhale, and look deep into the distance at the many other doors waiting to open beyond the one you just stepped through.*

*Look past all the doors until you come to the door with the word "Love" written on it.*

*Know this to be the door to your heart.*

*Understand how this is the door opening to all your grief and all your sorrow together with all your deep, abiding love.*

*Walk through this door and enter into a garden.*

*Find a place to sit quietly, stay for as long as you wish.*

*As you look around, be aware of all you see, sense, and smell.*

*Be aware of the peace and beauty in this garden. The Garden of Love and Loss.*

*Know this garden as the garden of your heart and of your undying love, the place of most painful grief and most abiding love, held together in peace and beauty within the silence and scent of this garden that belongs to you and is yours to tend.*

*Notice anything in your garden that needs attention.*

*Anything to be weeded, pruned, watered, sat beside.*

*Before you leave the garden, notice one flower. Linger with its color and scent.*

*Look into the center of the flower. See one word written there for you.*

*Place the one word in your heart. Carry it there as you leave the garden.*

*Know you can always return tend the garden and receive its peace that holds both your grief and your love.*

## In your journal

Write your journey through the doors of Love and Loss.

Is the door of loss close up or at a distance? Or both? Write.

Stay with your feelings of loss and love—write slowly.

Write on two facing pages. Title one page: "Loss." Title the other: "Love."

Write slowly, as feelings, images, and memories arise on each page.

Describe the garden you enter of loss and abiding love.

Draw the flower you found.

Write what was written for you in the middle of the flower.

# 48.

## *The human family becomes my family*

DEATH TEACHES US THAT WE ARE ALL ONE. We are not separate. We all live; we all love; we all have a heart that yearns, hurts, laughs, and cries. And we all die. Death teaches us this: If grief does not turn us to stone, we soften and look at one another in a new way. We know each one of us will lose loved ones, and we know death will come for us one day. Deeply understanding the impermanence of our lives moves us to take tender care of each other. We all belong to one another.

This coming to know the oneness of all beings opens compassion in us—the desire to touch a heart, ease a pain, lift someone up, care for one another. The veil of separateness begins to dissolve as we journey along The Path of Grief. We begin to feel connected beyond the limits of our own home, family, race, or country. In the land of grief, your heart transforms: You feel boundaries expand. When others hurt, you hurt, too. The venerable Vietnamese monk, Thich Nhat Hanh, who knew the grief of witnessing many of his people killed in war, calls this "inter-being," where we no longer feel separate from one another. In grieving, we grow aware of sharing birth, living a life, and dying into death.

Along the path of our grief journey, we come to inter-be.

*Debra, a mother whose teenage son died in an automobile accident five years ago brought me a photo from a magazine of a mother in Sudan holding her child in the midst of a drought: The child's stomach is swollen and his eyes, wide with hunger and fear, stare into the face of his helpless mother.*

*Debra wept, head bent, as she sat holding the picture. We sat silently together, in mourning for this mother and child, bewildered that such a thing could happen. We sat with this mother and child. We sat with all the mothers and all the children that are unprotected. We felt heartbreak. We shed tears. Debra's tears for the mothers and the children were one with her tears for her own son.*

*We sat with the ache in our hearts for the suffering of the innocent. Finally, Debra said, "I feel this mother's pain, I'm crying the tears she is too stricken to cry. She is going to bury her child soon. I want to stand beside her, as others stood beside me when my son died. I want to be there for her when her baby dies. That is what my heart wants to do. My heart knows her heart."*

*I felt Debra's longing to be there for this mother and her child. I, too, felt the sorrow, the ache to enter the photograph, to rush to where they are, to bring them what they need, to carry them to safety, to care for them.*

We are all one, we are all vulnerable, we are each touched with the gift of life, we will all experience loss and death, and there is much we can do to make life better for all of us. If only the heads of state, whose hands sign the papers for war and the taking of sacred life, could look into the faces of the mothers who have lost their children until they cry and their hearts crack open. If only they would take hold of the hands of the grieving mothers and look into their broken hearts until the ancient tribal acts of revenge dissolve into one heart.

Debra could not go to Sudan to help. Nor could I. But, all around us, in our own families, among our friends, and in our communities, there are calls for small and not-so-small acts of kindness: a smile; a touch; a contribution; a meal; a sitting with babies of addicted mothers in nurseries waiting to be held, rocked, sung to; elders sitting alone in nursing homes waiting for someone to visit them; abandoned animals waiting in shelters for a new home; a refugee needing help to make a new home, a sick neighbor receiving the care of a pot of soup; a harried clerk needing a warm smile and a sincere "Thank you."

Some of you, awakened by your grief to our common bonds, will hear the call to serve others, and possibly find your way to Sudan, or to other distant lands in need of volunteers and skilled workers.

Others of us will find our calling closer to home.

In becoming a psychologist and a trauma and grief therapist, I have been graced with the ground on which to sit with my human family, witness to the miraculous ways of the human spirit, deeply touched as the frozen places of suffering, slowly thaw into sacred tears, and life, once again, begins to flow through grief. I see the wonder of a tender, sad smile beginning to thaw a grief-frozen face. I hear my heart whisper, "Thank you, life, for returning to this grieving soul."

As you travel through your grief, may you receive the gift of loving-kindness for all creation.

May you come to treasure the fragility of life in all its beauty.

On your grief journey, may you grow keenly aware of life's brevity.

May you hear your particular call to serve life as only you can.

## Guided meditation: Contemplating compassion for all life

*Open your hands and cup them.*

*Raise up the cup of your hands.*

*Feel and sense the energies of compassion pulsating in your hands.*

*Know this as the cup of your compassion for all things, all people.*

*Can you see a color suffusing the energy of compassion in the cup of your hands?*

*Indigo? Scarlett? Rose? Gold? White?*

*Know this as the color of your deep heart feelings of compassion and loving kindness.*

*Now, allow the cup of your hands to touch these energies of compassion for all things, for all people deep in the center of your heart.*

*Know your compassion will always sit in your heart and in the cup of your hands.*

*Trust that your compassion for your self and others will always wait for you to return when it feels lost to you.*

*Wear or carry with you something in the color of your compassion for all life.*

*Choose a small piece of jewelry, a scarf, a piece of clothing, a touchstone to remind you to go out from and return to your heart of compassion as you move through your day.*

*As you sit and breathe, send the compassion of your heart out to your loved ones, to those familiar to you to your kindred spirits.*

*Breathing in, see their foibles breathe out your compassion. In the pause, see how flawed we each are.*

*Being with your breathing, see someone who is different from you, who dresses differently, thinks differently.*

*Send your compassion to this "other," to this stranger, know how their time here is fleeting.*

*Know how they are just like you, wanting a good life.*

*Send compassion to your own fear and distrust, to your impulse to turn away from to be rid of the other, including those parts of yourself about which you say, "This is not me."*

*Take these others into the circle of your heart.*

*Know their humanity as your own, how they, too, wish for a simple, good life.*

*Bless them and wish for them peace and happiness, good health, freedom from suffering.*

*Wish for them and for yourself a good life and a good death.*

*Invite them to sit at the table with you inside the home of your heart.*

*May we send blessings of peace out into the world to everyone, everywhere.*

*May we become peace within.*

*May we stop and notice moments of peace and smile the smile of peace.*

*May we sense our loved ones who are gone resting in the embrace of a great peace and a great love.*

## *In your journal*

In your place of solitude, with your journal nearby, let yourself settle into your breathing.

Be aware of your body and your breathing.

Take your time and come to rest in the space between your inhalation and exhalation.

In the resting space, be aware of anyone close to you, or of someone at a distance, a person, a whole people, a country, who is "other" to you, sensed as threatening, with whom you feel unsafe.

Be aware of and write your body senses, your feelings, into your journal. Let them arise.

Pause as you write, to sense, feel, and be aware of your body.

Then, sit again with your breathing and bring compassion to your own feelings, to your longing for safety, for whatever arises in you as an alive need.

Write about whatever is felt and wants to be known in your feelings.

Place a hand on these feelings where they sit in your body.

Give your compassion to your needs and sacred longings.

Now, see in front of you the other. Sense their needs and longings. Take your time. Breathe.

Sense and feel any compassion you can bring to them and their humanity. Take your time.

Write of any sense of inter-being you may feel, how you are the same, how you each want to live beyond fear, made a good life, have suffered loss and treasured love.

And if you cannot feel a sense of inter-being with this other, let yourself feel compassion for this and write about it.

Know how this spiritual practice of inter-being takes its time.

# 49.

## *The planet becomes my concern*

VIETNAMESE MONK THICH NHAT HANH teaches that the trees are our lungs, the sun is our heart, and everything on this planet is connected to everything else. We are all one body: skies, oceans, fish, forests, animals, humans, and if one part of this body is ill, it affects every other part. The fabric of this planet, this incredible universe, is woven together, every strand indispensable to the whole.

Sometimes, we can sense the moan of Mother Earth's grief over the losses she has suffered, with the death of her creatures, her air, her waters and land, calling to us to sit and connect with her, to hear her heart of grief.

When death comes into our life, loss and grief teach us just how sacred every strand of life is. When we see how we have neglected to care for life on our planet, when we see what we have done to our air, water, the ozone layer, rain forests, and oceans, we feel the pain keenly. Because our journey through loss and grief has intensified our heart's sensitivity to the sacredness of all life, we ask, what can we do to nurture and support our planet, what can we do to protect it from harm?

Once we are cracked open by knowing death and grief, knowing the impermanence and vulnerability of all living things, we can no longer continue to believe we are separate from one another or our planet.

We can try to ignore our interconnectedness and keep our hearts closed, but somehow, when the veil of separateness drops away, and we see ourselves a part of everything—all life—the whole front of our soft animal body opens to the vulnerable body of our world. Even a small drop of water seen with the heart is a precious pearl.

*I am walking around the Taos Pueblo, where Native Americans have lived for 900 years. I am with a group of visitors being led by a young Native American woman.*

*We come to a stream of water flowing down from a beautiful mountain. She points to the mountain and says, "That is a sacred mountain. Only our elders are allowed to climb this mountain once a year for religious ceremonies. This stream is one of the only pure streams in the state, and it is our duty to take care of it."*

*Returning from our tour of the reservation, and once again standing at the stream, I ask our guide if it would be all right to drink from it. She says yes. I go down to the stream, kneel, cup my hands, and lift the pure, sparkling water to my mouth. I drink it, touch my face with it, put it to my eyelids. And then, suddenly, I burst out crying.*

*I am sobbing with the sudden knowing of how the pristine beauty of this water is flowing forth from the one into the arms of Mother Earth. The earth's purity and our sacred trust to honor and preserve all that lives on this planet has pierced my soul. I am in awe of the inter-being of the water, and the mountain, and the light, and the animals, and how the people here live in cherishing intimacy with Mother*

*Earth.*

*Still standing at the stream, in this moment of knowing, I sense the light of my daughter circulating in the light of this land.*

As we travel the terrain of grief, sometimes we stand before the thin curtain that separates life and death. In that brief moment, when this curtain flutters open, we are given a glimpse of how love transitions from here to there, from life to death. In that flashing glimpse of timeless time, we glean the great mystery out of which each precious life flows and to which it returns.

May we, when the curtain closes, not forget the deeper reality: There is no separation between the worlds, only the flowing forth of creation, lighting the cells of every living thing, every living thing precious.

May we know this deeply, live mindfully of our inter-being, our oneness with every living thing.

May life and death, love and loss teach us that, like a mother with her child, it is for us to take care of life.

May we tend the pulse and beauty, the aliveness, the joy and the ache of pain that is part of all that is filled with the breath of life.

## Guided meditation: Grief teaches me I am part of all that is

*Close your eyes focus your attention on your breathing.*
*As you breathe quietly, feel your body becoming relaxed,*
*your muscles, organs, skin, neck, back, all of you, easing, relaxing.*

*Allow yourself to breathe gently, as you breathe enter the space of a waking dream.*

*In your dream, see that it is night.*

*See a mountain lit by a full moon.*

*See an antelope standing solitary on the mountaintop.*

*See the antelope, head lifted, looking up at the moon and a vast star-lit sky.*

*In your waking dream, be aware of an immense stillness.*

*Know this stillness to be the great silence of the universe.*

*In your dream, know how this mountaintop is home to the antelope.*

*Sense how she is one of the ancestors.*

*See her standing there, so still, in deep meditation.*

*See her large antlers reaching up into the heavens.*

*See how they are thin, and delicate, and filled with great electrical power.*

*In your dream, know how her antlers make contact with the hidden spheres of the great love that give life to everything on our planet.*

*Know how the antelope is always there on top of the mountain.*

*See how its body is aglow in the moonlight as it watches over life on this earth.*

*Sense how the antelope beholds the seamless web of creation.*

*Know how, with its antlers, the antelope brings down grace to heal what has been hurt by human abuse, of neglect, of overuse, to restore all that is living here to wholeness and holiness.*

*In your dream, know how you are like the antelope on the mountaintop.*

*Know how there is no difference between you and everyone and everything that lives and dies, how you are a part of the exquisite, sensitive balance of creation.*

*Be there on the mountain, feel your soft heart space in contact with all that is.*

*Sense your hands and heart reach like antenna to touch every living strand of creation.*

*May you abide in knowing how your oneness with and your care for all living things gives honor to the life of your loved one who has departed this life and yet goes on as part of the web of all that ever was and all that will ever be.*

## In your journal

Write your meditation as a dream, tell as many details as you can.

As you write, feel and sense yourself on the mountain.

Sense the antlers of the antelope, how they make contact with the heavens.

Be the antelope, living always on top of the mountain.

Feel your connection with the ancestors and with the hidden spaces of creation and how you are devoted to protecting all that lives.

Connect with that place in yourself that has even a drop of the essence of antelope.

Write about that.

Write about living from that drop of ancestor spirit into your life.

Sense if this drop of connection to and protection of life carries your loved one's essence.

Write.

# 50.

## *I live knowing I will die*

WHEN A JEWISH MAN MARRIES, he receives a white coat: It is the same coat he will be buried in. Built into this ritual is a reminder, an awareness, of the necessity for a life-long intimate relationship with the cycle of life and death. At the doorways of Buddhist dwellings, there hangs a skull to be seen as a person goes out from and returns home, reminded of death at the threshold. Such rituals interconnecting life and death, remind us how death is a real, inevitable, and inescapable part of life. In forgetting about death, we lose a vital and necessary meeting with life.

When someone close to us dies unexpectedly, we meet death on intimate terms. The veil of illusion drops. We are thrown across the boundary separating us from death. We are thrown up against death—smell it, taste it, feel it, and begin to live with it every day. Confronting the death of a beloved becomes a ritual of passage into knowing how the wheel of death and birth, living and dying, turn together in a never-ending circle.

Don Juan Matus, a Yaqui Mexican spiritual teacher, told his student, American anthropologist and author Carlos Castaneda, to live always with death sitting on his left shoulder. To live with death as an equal partner and teacher in our life allows us to live life more fully and authentically. When we live without the keen awareness that we could die at any moment, we are more likely to spend our precious time mired down in daily routines, worrying about what other people think of us, and putting off, deferring our dreams. Connections with dear ones delayed, visits postponed, passions ignored, love unexpressed, because we forget the urgency to live with the keen commitment to what is really important to us.

*Marvin is 68 years old and is acutely aware that he will soon turn three score and 10.*

*His wife Mary has major responsibility for their contact with children and grandchildren. Marvin, a successful businessman, spends much of his free time in their finished basement, playing piano. He confides to me that his wife resents his absence. Recently, Marvin has begun share his sadness for withdrawing himself, for being too absorbed in his business successes.*

*He says, "I look at her and see that she misses my touching her hand or putting my arm around her. I see how vulnerable she is and how much she longs for me to be there, really be there. I want my wife to have that intimacy. And I long to have that myself before I turn 70."*

*Death truly sits on Marvin's left shoulder, asking, "Marvin, how shall you live this day, this moment? What is your living here for?"*

The sense of impermanence we come know when facing death and loss and journeying along The Path of Grief, arouses in us the longing and an imperative to live from our true center, to follow our true North.

This is the only diamond we really own, the diamond of our heart's deep knowing of why we are here, the only diamond that cannot be destroyed. The diamond waits in the center of our heart for us to return, for surely it knows how, in our frailty, we shall become lost from our center again and again.

All kinds of things will call us away. But, because on the path of loss and love, we have come to know of the brevity of life, we long to live the true life we came here to live. It is amazing to me that the longing to live from our center arises out of our journey through grief. How loss and grief and love and impermanence become our teachers to truly live before we die is the amazing grace that opens out of our grief journey.

May we always turn and return to the land of our heart. May we hear our heart calling us back when we stray, and stray we will.

May we know why we are here in this life, may we remember to serve our calling before death comes calling for us.

## Guided meditation: Entering the field of your life

*Come to your breathing.*

*Be aware of your breath coming and going, like the clouds coming and going.*

*Be with your breath, rising, and falling, and waiting for the next breath rising out of emptiness.*

*As you breathe out, allow your exhalation to become long. Let your exhalation become a path that you are walking on. This path is known only to you.*

*It is the path of your precious life, yours to walk alone. Feel the solid ground under your feet.*

*Follow along the path until you see a wide-open field.*

*Now you are there, in the wide-open field of turning, and returning, and realigning your life to the truth of your heart.*

*Be aware of all you see, and sense, and feel in your field.*

*Sense how, in the field, time has slowed down. How you are far from the busy, speeding time of your daily life.*

*Sense how, in your field, you are a part of the sacred rhythm of creation, breathing with every living thing, with every blade of grass, breathing in the stilled emptiness out of which all life is renewed.*

*Know how you are standing in the field of your life.*

*Know how you are called by your heart to stand in the field of your life.*

*Feel how you have come here to search for the turning and returning of your soul to its true living, its destiny.*

*As you stand in the field, be aware of how the good earth nourishes you so that you can stand solid and gather all your courage and all your strength to turn what needs to be turned and returned in your life.*

*Lift your head and notice the heavens open to you.*

*You may even see a gate opening to the deepest parts of the heavens.*

*Feel and know how the gates of heaven are open for you, waiting to hear the longing of your heart.*

*Allow the calls of your longing to rise up to the heavens that are open for you.*

*Be aware of how your breath, carrying your calls, forms a bridge of breath all the way up to the heavens.*

*Be aware of how the bridge of your breath's call is heard by an angel in the heavens who watches over your life.*

*Call aloud with all your might and the courage of your*

*heart, trusting that you will be heard.*

*Now, be still in the field of your life. Rest in knowing you have done what you came to do, to renew your bridge between heaven and earth, to receive the sacred guidance for your life to live.*

*Listen in the stilled emptiness until you hear.*

*In the stillness, let yourself hear one or two words that come to you across the bridge of breath between you and the heavens.*

*Take this word. Place it somewhere in your body to be carried by you, an anchor in your body and heart and soul for your life.*

*Whisper the word or words three times, know how they are entering you to unfold your life, your words, and your deeds.*

*Then, be still and hear the heavens whisper them back to you.*

*Feel your words sealed into your heart and under your tongue, ready to guide you to live your life in reverence for your loved one who is gone and for all of life.*

## *In your journal*

In your journal, simply write the words the came across the bridge of your breath.

Write them slowly. Write them as a prayer. As a meditation.

Write slowly, breathing each word or your one word.

Then sit silently. Be aware of the saliva under your tongue.

Place your word or words into the saliva and let the word for your life come to rest under your tongue.

Know how your speech will be for life.

And the word or words in your heart, let yourself know how they will be for your actions.

Know how your field is ever there for you to return to.

Know how your loved one is happy for you, that you are living from your sacred being.

Know how death on your left shoulder is happy to witness you harvesting your living.

# 51.

## *I try to understand this life*

AS I NEAR THE COMPLETION OF THIS BOOK, which has felt like a long letter to you, I realize it has also been a letter to myself, for whatever I have tried to give to you, I, too, am in need of receiving.

As I write, my heart tries to understand, to penetrate the mystery of this life I have been given. Even now, I see the beginning of the end. I have turned 80. I have become wrinkled, and I will become frail, and I am keenly aware I will die, sooner rather than later. I will return to dust and be no more in this physical body. These are the stark, unadorned realities I see with my heart. At times, I close my heart to seeing unadorned reality. Sometimes, I do not want to see, do not want it to be so. I do not want to practice awareness of this life, this dying, this death.

From my time spent with death—standing alongside death with my precious daughter, my dear friends, my father and mother, and beloved

dogs—sitting beside clients who are losing and mourning loved ones—
I carry profound sorrow and profound awe. That those I've loved have
been so alive in my life and then so suddenly gone missing, leaves me
aching and bewildered: I can no longer see, touch, hear them, or feel
their presence, except in dreams or in those amazing moments when
they vividly return for a time to my heart and memory, only to fade
like a dream.

As I look out over the mountains into vast space, I look for them,
I miss them, I smile remembering them. But my memories are not all I
carry from my life with them, from my sharing in their death. I also
carry a profound experience of light, especially at the moment Leslie
died, when light and death became teachers. When my daughter's spirit
left her body, I was surrounded by a soft, luminous, quietly pulsating
light that penetrated everything, everywhere, parting the veils to a great
mystery.

I ask myself, what is this light? What is the power of this light that
is still with me after all these years?

In its presence, I sit in silence, bow with awe before it. I sense it is
the light of the great sea of creation, what the Kabbalists call "Ayin,"
what the Buddhists call "Śūnyatā," the formless void that was there
before any form of creation existed, the pure land of light, the great
womb of love, out of which all form comes and to which all form returns. To write about the light I have experienced, the light that is
within us, and all around us, I need these words, which may sound
philosophical, but truly they are the only words I can take hold of to
utter what I have no words for.

And so, I sit, looking out at the mountains, asking the questions:
Who am I? Who are you? Where did we come from and where will
we go? Where are the people we loved and lost? I do not know. None
of us knows. We each make up our story to tether us in the cloud of

unknowing. In this moment, writing to you, in my story, all I know is that birth is not really a beginning and death is not really an end.

Death is the end only of a particular form, a particular body, and way of being. The loss of that form, the loss of our loved ones, is to us heartbreaking, as it must be.

My journey on The Path of Grief has touched me with a knowing that we can live our lives guided by a sense of awe and reverence for the sacred mystery of life and death until it is our time to return to the light. I do not know this with my mind, my intellect; I know this only through this journey that opened my heart and senses to the Light.

As I sit here writing, I understand why I sense my daughter's presence when I hear a bird sing or see a flash of sunlight. The light that she is, the clay that she was, is now part of the earth, nourishing all that continues to live and grow. She is part of the birdsong. She always was. And so are we. Each of us, all that we are, every particle of our being is a part of the invisible ever-present, ever-flowing ocean of being.

The same is true of all our loved ones who are no longer here with us. They, too, are one with all that is. Their light is in the light of the sun and the soft glow of the moon. Their clay is in the clay of the earth. This I learned from the life and the death of my daughter.

In rare moments, we, who are alive, can sense ourselves vibrating with all the forms and energies of life, we can feel our energy a part of all energy throughout all time and all creation. We die, but then, nothing dies. It all goes on. We are born, but then nothing is born; it has always been. Only our forms are forever changing. Only love is changing, forever changing its name.

At 80, I live with two hands open: One hand holds the never-ending grief for those who are gone while the other holds the unending being of life.

# Guided meditation: Breathing the mystery

*Sit in stillness. Be aware of your breathing.*

*Breathe in, breathe out.*

*Be aware of the quiet space between your breaths.*

*Sense and feel the miracle of breathing, the mystery of your breath coming and going.*

*How it will come and go until your last breath.*

*As you sit in stillness, know that in the deep soil of your grieving has been planted a seed of understanding within you.*

*Know that deep within your heart, this seed endures, sometimes dormant, hidden in darkness, at other times in bloom, igniting your awareness with a sudden flash of knowing light.*

*Know how this seed is planted deep in your heart to reveal the mystery of life and death:*

*"I am dust. I am light. I die and my form changes, but love never changes; I am always love.*

*Light never changes; I am always light.*

*Light pouring into form, light pouring out of form.*

*Light returning to light."*

*Do not try to understand this mystery with your mind.*

*You will not, none of us ever will.*

*Simply breathe, trust, understand with your heart.*

*Behold the mystery of your breath and the mystery of all life breathing with you.*

*On your journey through grief, may you find your very own understanding of life and death.*

*May you know, too, how life and death are beyond your understanding.*

*May you go on with both a deep understanding of life and death and with a sense of wonder for what is beyond your understanding.*

## *In your journal*

As you sit quietly, be aware of the feelings that arise in this meditation.

Let yourself write of your own sense of life and death.

Write of what you understand and of what you do not, no matter how you try.

Are there images that appear for you when you hear the words "life" and "death?"

Pause to see and sense these images.

Write about them.

Use your colors to draw anything that comes to you from this meditation.

Perhaps colors will catch your eye as you reread the meditation and find yourself pausing at certain images and words.

# 52.

## *Life and death go on and on*

MY MOTHER DIED AT AGE 94. Ten years after her first stroke, she went in peace. She was a powerful spirit and I still feel her presence. I miss her, and I do not know where she has gone. One moment she was here, the next she was nowhere. She is somewhere. Only tell me, where? I will always be her child and I will always wonder like a child and ask the questions a child asks. As my mother entered the last transition of her life, I recall feeling like the four-year-old granddaughter of my friend Helen: *Helen finds a dead dragonfly in her house. It seems beautiful to her. She leaves it on the table where she found it. The sun streams through the window, lighting the dragonfly's wings like a rainbow. When Helen's granddaughter comes to visit, she sees the dragonfly on the table. "Why can't it fly?" she asks. "It's dead," Helen tells her. This begins months of Joy's incessant questions about death. "What is death? Are you going to die? Am I going to die? Where do you go? Will I ever see you again?" One night, Joy wakes, pleading: "Please, Mommy. Please, Daddy, please let's all die together. I don't want to die alone. I don't know how to do it by myself!"*

It doesn't matter that we understand each one of us must die alone, our heartbreaking question is still there: "My loved one, can you do this alone, for I cannot do it with you. I cannot go along to comfort you." All I could do was sit beside my mother as she was dying. My hand on her cheek, I sang her story, in the same way I sang to my daughter at bedtime: "You are a beautiful mother, a brave mother, a strong mother, you did your very best." It was all finally true. Each time I reached into the well of my heart, all I could find was love, my mother looking up at me with wide-open eyes, drinking in the music of love. Love was what remained, that was the gift to ease her journey and to comfort my own.

In a few years, I will be the age of my mother when she had her first stroke. I am graced with good health now, but the wheel turns toward my death. I begin to grieve the end of my life. And so, I question myself: Will I be able to do my dying well? How shall I practice? How shall I become simple, until. . .

My friend Devra lives on a beautiful lake. It is such a calming feeling to slowly ease off the dock and surrender into the deep, velvet waters. Somehow, I see entering the great sea of death as such a surrendering, an easing into the deep vast still sea of silence, into the vast ocean of love. And so, I am practicing.

I wish my daughter had lived to be at my side when I am dying, to hold my hand, to sing to my soul, as I sail away, as I was able to do for my mother. But that will not be. Who knows, perhaps Leslie will be there, holding my hand as I glide into the great silence, into that place where "it never rains and never snows, and the light always shines." But I know, when it is my time, other loved ones will be beside me, holding my hand, touching my cheek, singing my soul song to me as I drift away.

For now, all I can do is wonder what death will be like when it comes, wonder without answers about the mystery of life and death. Children and philosophers ask the same questions, young and old alike struggle to find the answers. I wonder: Why don't we who have lived to become elders have more answers or bring more to the questions?

I shrug my shoulders. My eyes widen. I do not know if living longer, knowing more, perhaps even having a touch of wisdom, brings anything more to our quest to understand the unfathomable mysterious turnings of life and death.

Perhaps the questions themselves are sufficient, all the questions that little Joy, and big Judith, and each one of us goes on asking in spite of our intuition that we will never know the answers until we get there.

May the aliveness of our sincere questions and our deep wonderings form a path of reverence and tenderness for each one of us.

## Guided meditation: Sitting with your questions for life and death

*Now, dear fellow pilgrim on The Path of Grief, as we come to the last pages of our journey through this book, let us sit in The Garden of Love and Loss together for a while.*

*Let us sit in the silence,*
*breathe the breath of life, in and out.*

*In the space of your silence, you may wish to sit with your questions and your feelings about life and death.*

*Sit with the feelings that arise in you as you hold your questions.*

*Take your time, breathe in and out. Pause.*

*Sit again with your questions, your feelings, your thoughts.*

## *In your journal*

What have you learned on your journey through the land of grief?

What seeds of deep knowing have grown from sitting with your loved one?

From sitting with death?

From journeying on The Path of Grief?

From breathing the mysterious breath of life?

Write your questions, and thoughts, and feelings into your journal.

Let the answers appear out of your meditative stillness.

Perhaps you can sit comfortably, accepting, holding the questions without answers.

Perhaps you feel the questions themselves are sufficient and you can go on living them.

Perhaps the questions you sit with open a sense of awe and deepen your reverence for life.

If words come, let them come and write them in your journal.

If no words come, sit in the open space of your unformed questions and feelings.

We do not always need answers. We cannot always have them.

May we each accept the ultimate simplicity of sitting silently with mystery beyond words.

Sometimes, the questions themselves offer us a deep encounter with of life and death

May we be breathed by our questions.

May we find healing and comfort in living our questions with simplicity and sincerity.

# Songlines

WHEN I HEARD OF THE SONGLINES of the Indigenous People of Australia, I understood them to be places where they crossed the desert without the aid of map or compass. Perhaps something like our journey through the land of grief. As we travel, every aspect of our journey forms lines of silent song into existence across our souls and along our faces.

We know one another by the songlines that cross our faces: lines of sorrow, of smiles, of tears, of bewilderment, of searching, of solitude, of wonder—all the lines formed by the journey we have taken along The Path of Grief.

Songlines formed on our faces by our courage to keep going through the darkest of places.

Songlines from finding ourselves touched by unexpected grace flowing from mysterious, hidden, sacred places.

Songlines of kindness from others and for others because we know how each life is as fragile and each journey as vulnerable as our own.

Songlines of deep compassion for those who do not find their way, who remain alone with their grief.

My hope is that we see the songlines of love and mercy upon one another's faces, that we carry hard-earned blessings to give one another, wherever we may be.

# In closing

I HAVE NEVER BEEN SURE WHAT PRAYER IS. When I hear that someone prays, I secretly wonder what that means but am too embarrassed to ask, thinking everyone but me knows.

Someone once said that to pray is to become very quiet and listen very deeply until something comes.

This makes sense to me: to enter silence, to listen deeply, until we hear. As we come to the closing of this journey, I still myself, enter the silence of what I call the great love and sit quietly until a small voice arises and whispers within my heart.

Through the reflections, guided meditations, and journal suggestions of this book, we have walked alone and together on The Path of Grief, and we have sat alone and together in The Garden of Love and Loss. Now, as we close our journey, it feels fitting to sit in silence, to listen, to hear our prayers for going on.

Below, I offer what I hear in the stillness of my heart that helps me continue along my path of love and loss.

*Dear Breath of Life,*

*Please hold my hope, hold my deep desire to love and serve life.*

*Please let this book give healing to even one person on their path of grief.*

*Please hold my darkness, tattered remnants of my grief.*

*Please place a star within my heart to guide my way when I become lost.*

*Help me know my fullness. Forgive me my emptiness.*

*May my living shine forth the essence of my departed loved ones who are ever with me.*

*Help me carry gently the places within still wrapped in frozen grief.*

*Help me remember the unbreakable circle of love and life.*

*Help me to have compassion for all that is broken and a sense of wide-eyed wonder for all that is whole.*

*And, when it is my time to die, may my memory be for a blessing, for that will mean I had lived and touched others in some good way.*

I invite you to sit in silence until the words arise from your heart to speak and write your personal prayer for going on. If it feels right, you may want to share it with someone close.

May your prayer bring you comfort and healing, renewal and hope, and guide your way.


HEAVEN

All afternoon the sprinkler
ticks and sprays,
ticks and sprays
in lazy rounds,
trailing a feather of mist
a feather of mist. When I turn it off,
the cicadas keep up their own dry rain,
passing on high from limb to limb.
I don't know what has shocked me more,
that you are gone, that I am still here,
that there is music after the end.

—*David Baker*

## ACKNOWLEDGMENTS

I thank my teacher of Imagination, Mme. Collette Aboulker-Muscat, may her memory be a blessing. I first entered Collette's Jerusalem garden, behind the blue gate, in 1980 to find a true home for my heart's work in journeying through the space and time of imagination, to reach and be touched by unexpected sources of spiritual healing and renewal. Behind the blue gate I sat with friends and colleagues, who also travelled from the States to study with Collette. I thank Drs. Judy Besserman, Francis Clifton, and Gerald Epstein for the sense of community in carrying forward Collette's teachings, each in your own way and for sharing the vast pool of her imaginal journeys. Many of the meditations of this book belong to that collective pool. I am grateful to creatively adapt them for those who are grieving.

I thank the following people for giving of their time in reading the several iterations of the manuscript of this book. Thank you, Devra Black, MSW; Laura Himmelstein, MSW; Alexis Johnson, PhD; Leigh Rosoff; Ginny Vreeland; and Susan Walton, MSW.

Thank you, Kathleen Hughes, for sensitively editing the first version of this book.

Thank you, Nancy Eichorn, for creatively walking with me through continued editing.

Thank you, Lia Dangelico, for your expertise in representation and copy-editing—and for your patience with my technical illiteracy! You are just who I needed!

Thank you, Linda Blachman, dear forever friend, for your steadfast presence in reading and editing. Your gifts as writer and editor are pure gold.

Thank you, Leigh Rossoff, for the offering of your beautiful photo of the blades of grass.  For so long, I have passed it hanging in my home, seeing the blades of grass touched by tears of mourning and touched by the dew drops of a new day.

Thank you, Barry Sheinkopf, publisher of Full Court Press, for the superb guidance you have given to me and for your expertise in preparing this book for publication.  Thank you for your devotion to the writer and for knowing how to get the job done in such a supportive and seamless way.  And I love the finished product!

There are three teachers I wish to thank.  Although I have never met them, each deeply inspires me:

Thich Nhat Hahn, Buddhist teacher, thank you for your teachings of inter-being, the Oneness of all that is, and for your smile of peace, which I imagine was hard-earned given the suffering of your country, Vietnam.

Thank you, Emanuel Levinas, Jewish philosopher, who spent six years in a German work camp.  He lost his mother, father, and siblings.  His wife and daughter, given refuge in a monastery, survived.  After his release, on a spring day, he dressed up and went to a Paris café, where an elderly man held the door for him.  Levinas looked into the face of the man, said "Thank you, Mercy."  He wrote that to look into the face of the other is to see utter vulnerability, to be called to care for the sacred otherness of the other.

I thank the British psychoanalyst Donald W. Winnicott, and Jungian analyst Ann Ulanov, who taught me that it is possible to take the daunting journey, with the support of others, through in-between spaces, not knowing what may be at the other end, being amazed to open to new being and new beginnings.  They, along with friends, family, teachers, and therapists helped me abide in the in-between dark places of loss, to bear not knowing if new life would ever touch me, to find my heart touched by the sacredness of life shining forth as if for the first time.

I thank my friends and family for supporting my writing. Thank you, Anna Maria Beggeman and Mike Morter for the gift to write in the beauty and peace of Heart Space.

Finally, I thank the fields of white pages, beckoning me to find words when I thought there were none, words that shaped a Garden of Love and Loss.

## ABOUT THE AUTHOR

Judith Sarah Schmidt is a licensed clinical psychologist who has been in private practice since 1992 in Westchester County, New York. She studied Waking Dream Therapy with Collette Aboulker Muscat in Jerusalem. As a senior imagery, dream, and trauma therapist, she is informed and inspired by Winnicott, Jung, Buddhist, and Jewish spirituality. She integrates depth and imaginal psychotherapy and the restorative language of the body, and works with those who are in life transition and those who suffer from traumatic loss and bereavement. She cherishes those sacred moments of healing that arise like surprises from within the creative core of wholeness to restore the broken heart of grief.

Dr. Schmidt is co-director of The Center for Intentional Living (*www.intentionalliving.com*), an experiential learning community for mental health and healing arts professionals. The Three Year Professional Enrichment Program explores psycho-spiritual development across the life span, from early childhood through adulthood, culminating in the process of conscious ageing and dying. Over the past thirty years, she has taught in the United States, the Netherlands, Switzerland, Croatia and Italy.

She has published "Longing for the Blessing" and numerous poems in a variety of journals. She is currently at work on a spiritual memoir spanning the sudden, untimely death of her daughter at four years old through the years of growing into aging and facing her mortality. This memoir focuses on the powerful place dreams have in raising up the grieving soul to the sacredness of all living being.

CPSIA information can be obtained
at www.ICGtesting.com
Printed in the USA
LVHW090757031120
670551LV00004B/282